ADVENTURES WITH ATOMS AND MOLECULES

BOOK II

CHEMISTRY EXPERIMENTS FOR YOUNG PEOPLE

ROBERT C. MEBANE

THOMAS R. RYBOLT

Enslow Publishers, Inc.

44 Fadem Road   PO Box 38
Box 699   Aldershot
Springfield, NJ 07081   Hants GU12 6BP
USA   UK

ACKNOWLEDGMENT

We wish to thank Paula Watson and Sandy Zitkus-Mebane for their helpful comments, corrections, and suggestions during the preparation of this book. Our thanks also to Ronald I. Perkins of Greenwich High School, Connecticut, and to A. M. Sarquis of Miami University, Ohio, for reviewing the manuscript.

DEDICATION

This book is dedicated to Cyril Long Mebane and the memory of Howard Roy Rybolt. Our fathers believed in the power of education and the value of experience. We hope this book contributes to both.

Library of Congress Cataloging-in-Publication Data

Mebane, Robert C.
    Adventures with atoms and molecules.
    Includes indexes.
    Chemistry experiments for home or school demonstrate the properties and behavior of various kinds of atoms and molecules.
    1. Chemistry—Experiments—Juvenile literature. 2. Molecules—Experiments. 3. Experiments. I. Rybolt, Thomas R. II. Title.
QD38.M43 1985 540'.78 85-10177
ISBN 0-7660-1224-7 (bk. 1 pbk)
ISBN 0-7660-1225-5 (bk. 2 pbk)

Printed in the United States of America

10 9 8 7 6 5 4 3 2 1

Cover Illustration: © Corel Corporation

CONTENTS

FOREWORD

This book is the second in a series of chemistry experiments for young scientists. Continuing in the same format as the first book, it provides another set of safe, interesting, "NEAT," "WOW" experiments using common, everyday materials. Each activity concludes with a particle explanation and ideas for "Other things to try."

Although the experiments in this book are designed for students in fourth to sixth grade, many are appropriate for both younger and older children. Lower primary teachers will find a number of activities to use in the classroom; junior high school teachers will find this a valuable resource for individual work by students. Even adults will be intrigued with the answers to questions such as: Why is fish commonly served with lemon juice? Why is fresh pineapple never added to gelatin?

Both volumes are especially useful in providing students with ideas for science fair projects. In fact, my nephew won his elementary school science fair with a project on acid rain, an activity from the first volume of the series.

The first volume has become known as "the green book." I think that this volume will be received equally well and will become known as "the blue book."

The authors, once again, have provided parents and teachers with an ideal way to encourage young people to study chemistry using the kitchen as the laboratory.

Ronald I. Perkins

Assistant Director
Institute for Chemical Education
University of Wisconsin—Madison

INTRODUCTION

SCIENCE

Science is an adventure! Science is an adventure of asking questions and finding answers. Scientists are men and women who ask questions. Scientists answer questions by doing experiments and making observations. The results of their observations increase our knowledge and improve our understanding of the world around us.

Science is exciting because it never stops. There will always be new questions to ask. New questions lead to new experiments. New experiments lead to new knowledge and to new questions.

Experimentation is the heart of science. Experimentation lays the foundation upon which the basic principles of science are understood. You can gain a better feeling as to what science really is by doing science and experiencing science.

One way to share in the adventure of science is to do experiments. In our first book, Adventures With Atoms and Molecules, we presented thirty experiments and suggestions for over sixty additional activities. That book was a start, but there are many more experiments waiting to be done.

This book is a further collection of experiments which you can do at home or at school. These experiments will help you learn how to ask questions and find answers, and how to become a better observer. As you read about science and do experiments, you will learn more about yourself and your world. In asking questions and doing experiments, you will learn that observing and trying to understand the world around you is interesting and fun.

ATOMS, IONS, AND MOLECULES

One of the most important things that scientists have learned about our world is that EVERYTHING IS MADE OF ATOMS. Water, ice, air, sand, table salt, sugar, rocks, shoes, clothes, houses, bicycles, cars, leaves, trees, flowers, bees, ants, spiders, cows, horses, and people are all made of atoms.

Atoms are the basic building blocks of all things. There are 92 different kinds of natural atoms. A few additional atoms have been made by scientists in laboratories. Examples of natural atoms include: oxygen, hydrogen, carbon, nitrogen, mercury, gold, silver, sulfur, helium, chlorine, sodium, neon, nickel, copper, iron, silicon, phosphorus, aluminum, and calcium.

Atoms are found in all things. For example, a piece of aluminum foil is made of aluminum atoms. A diamond consists of carbon atoms. Sand is made of silicon and oxygen atoms. Table sugar is made of carbon, hydrogen, and oxygen atoms.

Molecules are combinations of tightly bound atoms. Water is a combination of hydrogen and oxygen atoms. Imagine you have a drop of water and you divide this drop into smaller and smaller drops. If you could continue to divide the drops enough times, you would eventually end up with a single water molecule. If you divide this water molecule any further, you would have two hydrogen atoms and one oxygen atom.

Scientists use models to represent molecules. Sometimes the models are made from small balls with the balls representing atoms. These models allow scientists to understand more about molecules. Models of a water molecule, a carbon dioxide molecule, an oxygen molecule, and a methane molecule are shown below. You can make similar models with marshmallows or gumdrops held together by toothpicks. Each marshmallow or gumdrop can represent one atom.

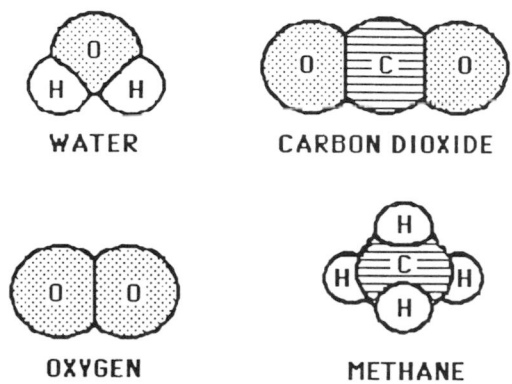

WATER   CARBON DIOXIDE

OXYGEN   METHANE

A water molecule is a combination of two hydrogen atoms and one oxygen atom. A carbon dioxide molecule is a combination of two oxygen atoms and one carbon atom. An oxygen molecule is a combination of two oxygen atoms. A methane molecule is a combination of four hydrogen atoms and one carbon atom. Natural gas consists of methane molecules.

Molecules that are made of only a few atoms are very small. Molecules are so small that you cannot see one even with the most powerful microscope. One drop of water contains two million quadrillion, (2,000,000,000,000,000,000,000) molecules. If you took two million quadrillion pennies and stacked one on top of the other, you would have three hundred thousand (300,000) stacks of pennies. Each stack would reach from the Sun to Pluto. Pluto is the planet in our solar system that is the greatest distance from the sun.

7

If you could magnify one drop of water to the size of the earth, each water molecule would be about the size of an orange.

Polymers are giant molecules made by combining many smaller molecules. Some polymer molecules may contain several million atoms. Important natural polymers include natural rubber, starch, and DNA. Rubber bands and some automobile tires are made of natural rubber. Starch is found in many foods. DNA is the molecule of heredity . Some important polymers made by scientists are nylon, which is used in making fabrics, polyethylene, which is used to make plastic bags and plastic bottles, and polystyrene, which is used in making styrofoam cups and insulation.

Atoms are made of smaller particles. These smaller particles are electrons, protons, and neutrons. Electrons are negatively charged and they spin around the nucleus. The nucleus is the center of the atom and contains protons and neutrons. Protons are positively charged and neutrons have no charge.

Atoms and molecules that contain a charge are called ions. Ions have either a positive charge or a negative charge. Positive ions have more protons than electrons. Negative ions have more electrons than protons. Sodium chloride, which is the chemical name for table salt, is made of positive sodium ions and negative chlorine ions.

Atoms or ions combine in chemical reactions to make molecules, metal alloys, or salts. Chemical reactions can also involve changing one molecule into a different molecule or breaking one molecule down into smaller molecules, atoms, or ions.

ABOUT THE EXPERIMENTS IN THIS BOOK

In this book we present thirty new experiments and suggestions for sixty-six additional activities. Many of the new experiments will show you how experimentation can be used to understand phenomena you encounter in your everyday life. Have you ever wondered how butter is made, how rust forms, or how eggs are colored? You will find out with the experiments in this book.

Each experiment is divided into five parts: 1) materials, 2) procedure, 3) observations, 4) discussion, and 5) other things to try. The materials are what you need to do the experiment. The procedure is what you do. The observations are what you see. The discussion explains what your observations tell you about atoms and molecules. The other things to try are additional questions and experiments which you can do to find out more about atoms and molecules.

This book is intended to be used and not just read. It is a guide toward doing, observing, and thinking science. The experimental activities described in this book are designed to give you an opportunity to experience science.

Do not worry about trying to understand everything about an experiment. You do not have to memorize words or meanings when you are first involved in science. You need to experience science first.

You do not have to do the experiments in the order they appear in the book. Each experimental activity has been written to stand completely alone. You will find that some experiments discuss the

9

same ideas. It will help you to learn and understand these ideas to see them more than once.

Not every experiment you do will work every time. Something may be different in the experiment when you do it. Repeat the experiment if it does not work and think about what may be different.

Not all of the experiments in this book give immediate results. Some experiments in this book will take some time to see observable results. Some of the experiments in this book may take a shorter time than that suggested in the experiment. Some experiments may take a longer time than suggested. You must be patient when doing experiments.

The drawings in this book were done using a computer graphics system. They are not intended to be a photographic or artistic substitution for what you will do and observe. The purpose of the drawings is to direct your attention to one or two key features of what you may expect to observe when you do each experiment.

SAFETY NOTE

WHEN YOU DO THESE EXPERIMENTS MAKE SURE YOU
1) Obtain an adult's permission before you do these
   experiments and activities.
2) Get an adult to watch you when you do an experiment.
   They enjoy seeing experiments too.
3) Follow the specific directions given for each experiment.
4) Clean up after each experiment.

And now the adventure continues . . .

DO LIKE CHARGES ATTRACT OR REPEL?

Materials

Two balloons

Thin thread

A meter stick or yardstick

Procedure

This experiment might not work if the air is humid or damp. Try to do this experiment when the air is dry. Usually the best time to do this experiment is in the winter.

Blow up two balloons and tie them closed. They should be about the same size. Using the thread, tie each balloon to the same end of the meter stick as shown in the drawing. The thread attaching the balloons to the meter stick should be about three feet long. Have a friend hold the meter stick. Observe the balloons.

Rub each balloon in your hair or on a sweater for about thirty seconds. Let the balloons drop and observe the balloons.

Move close to one of the balloons. What happens to it?

Rub your hands on each charged balloon suspended from the meter stick for fifteen seconds. Let the balloons drop. Observe the balloons again.

Observations

Do the balloons touch each other before you rub them in your hair or on a sweater? Do the balloons touch each other after you rub them in your hair or on a sweater? How far apart are the balloons? Do the balloons move farther apart if you rub them some more? Do the balloons move towards you as you move close to them? Do the balloons touch each other after you rub your hands on them?

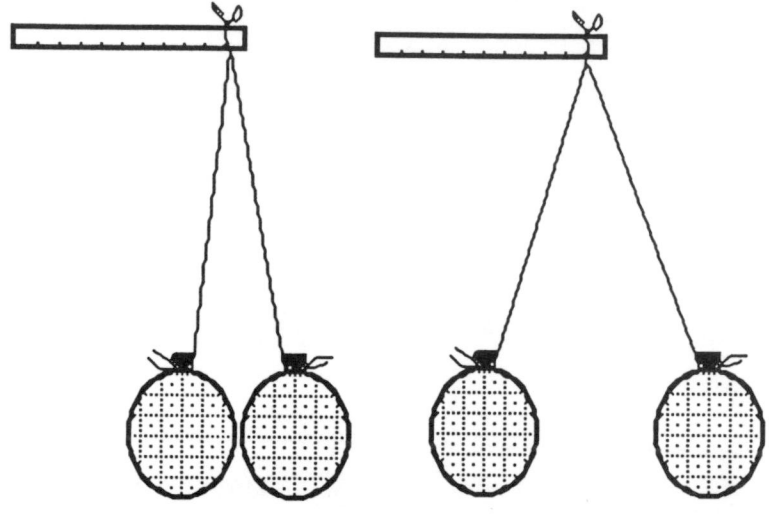

BEFORE CHARGING   AFTER CHARGING

Discussion

Atoms are made of tiny particles called electrons, protons and neutrons. Protons are positive particles, neutrons are neutral particles, and electrons are negative particles. Protons and neutrons are located in the center of atoms. The center of atoms is called the nucleus. Electrons move around the nucleus.

Electrons can sometimes be moved from one atom or molecule to another. When you rub a balloon in your hair or on a sweater, you rub electrons from your hair or sweater onto the balloon. The balloon is negatively charged because it has an excess of electrons. This is called static electricity. After you rub a balloon in your hair or sweater, your hair or sweater has fewer electrons and is positively charged.

The two balloons attached to the meter stick touch each other before you rub them in your hair because they are not charged. The balloons become negatively charged when you rub them in your hair or on a sweater. The balloons move apart after they are charged. They repel each other. Like charges repel each other. The negatively charged balloons are attracted to you when you move towards them because you are positively charged after you rub the balloons. Opposite charges attract each other. The balloons become uncharged when you rub them with your hands. Electrons move from the balloons onto you. You and the balloon become neutral. The balloons touch each other when they are neutral.

Have you ever been shocked by touching a doorknob or other object after shuffling your feet across a carpet? When you shuffle your feet across a carpet, you become charged. You become either positively charged or negatively charged depending on the shoes you are wearing and the type of carpet. With rubber soles and wool carpet, electrons move from the carpet onto you and you become negatively charged. If you are negatively charged and you touch a metal doorknob or other metal object, the extra electrons on you quickly move from you to the metal doorknob or other metal object. You feel a shock when this happens.

If you are positively charged and you touch a metal doorknob or other metal object, electrons from that object quickly move onto you.

Other things to try

Blow up a third balloon and tie it closed. Rub the balloon in your hair or on a sweater. Move the balloon close to one of the charged balloons suspended from the meter stick. Observe what happens. It should repel the charged balloon since like charges repel each other.

Tie three balloons to a meter stick. Charge each balloon by rubbing them in your hair or on a sweater. Have a friend help you charge them. Let the balloons go. Do the balloons form a triangular pattern?

Tie four balloons to a meter stick. Charge each balloon. Does one balloon stay in the middle and the others form a triangular pattern?

DOES AIR HAVE WEIGHT?

2

Materials

A flat wooden stick (about the size of a meter stick)

A large sheet of newspaper

A table

Procedure

The stick you use could get broken in this experiment. Make sure it is not a stick that must be saved.

Place the stick flat on the table. Move the stick so it hangs a few inches over the edge of the table. Stand to the side so you do not get hit by the stick. Hold your hand about six inches above the end of the stick. With your fist, rapidly hit the end of the stick that hangs over the edge of the table.

Now put the stick back on the table. Place the stick flat on the table. Move the stick so it hangs a few inches over the edge of the table. Cover the stick remaining on the table with a single, large sheet of newspaper. Smooth the newspaper so that it is pressed flat on the meter stick and on the table. With your fist, rapidly hit the end of the stick which hangs over the edge of the table.

You must hit the stick rapidly and not push slowly. If you push slowly, air slips under the paper and the stick will move easily. You cannot feel the weight of the air above the paper unless you hit the stick very quickly.

Observations

Is it easier to make the stick fly up in the air when it is covered or not covered with paper? Does the stick seem heavier when it is covered with newspaper?   Did it feel like there was a heavy weight on the stick when it was covered with paper?

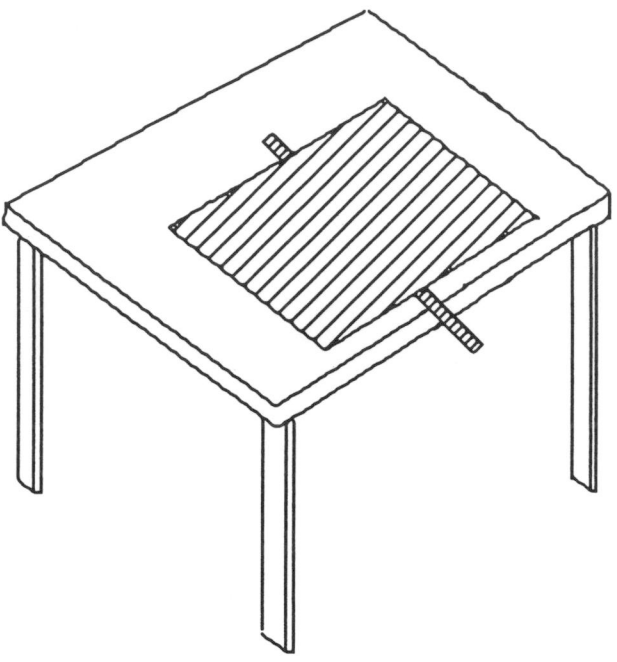

Discussion

Air is mostly made of nitrogen and oxygen molecules. Air also contains some argon, carbon dioxide, and water. Air is all around us and covers the surface of the earth. The same force of gravity that gives our bodies and everything on the earth weight also gives air weight.

In outer space there is no air, but for miles above our heads there is air. All that air is pulled down by gravity and pushes on every square inch with a weight of about fifteen pounds. We don't feel this weight because it is all around us. When you spread the paper flat on the table, there is air only on one side of the paper. The weight of the air on top of the paper pushes the paper down and helps to hold the stick in place when it is hit. The covered stick can seem very heavy when you hit it. The sheet of newspaper is light, but the air above it is heavy. A stick covered with paper moves very little when hit.

The weight of air is called the air pressure. Air pressure can be used to tell how high an airplane is above the earth. As a plane goes higher, there is less air and so the air pressure is less. The height above the earth is called the altitude. Altitude is measured with an altimeter. An altimeter measures the air pressure.

Other things to try

Fold the paper in half and cover the stick. Hit the stick and watch what happens. Using a smaller piece of paper should allow the stick to go higher when hit. Can you explain why?

You can do this same experiment with a foot ruler and a piece of notebook paper. You should not have to hit the ruler as hard because the ruler is shorter than the meter stick.

Have you ever seen a suction cup stuck on a wall? Can you explain what makes it stay there?

3 DO AIR MOLECULES MOVE FARTHER APART AS AIR IS WARMED?

Materials

An empty soft drink bottle   A quarter

A refrigerator freezer   A few drops of water

Procedure

Place an empty, uncapped soft drink bottle in a refrigerator freezer. You may use either a plastic or glass bottle. Wait ten minutes and remove the bottle from the freezer. Set the bottle on a table or other flat surface. Wet your finger and spread water across the quarter and around the top of the bottle. Slip the quarter on the bottle top. Make sure the quarter covers the mouth of the bottle. The water helps seal air inside the bottle. Watch the quarter for several minutes. Listen for any sounds.

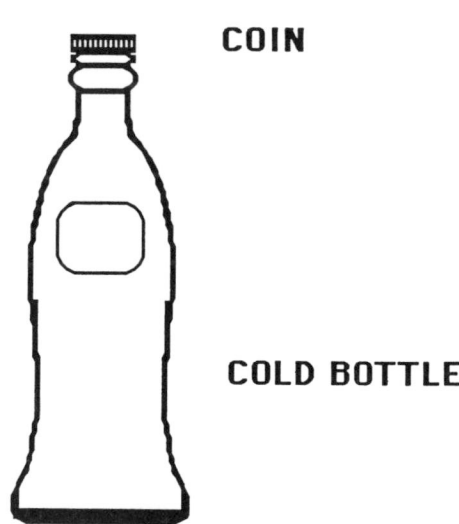

COIN

COLD BOTTLE

Observations

Does the quarter lift off the bottle? Does the quarter jump more than one time? When the quarter jumps, do you hear a click?

Discussion

Air is a gas mostly made of molecules of nitrogen and oxygen. Air also contains argon, carbon dioxide, and water. Air molecules are very small. These air molecules are much too small to see. There are spaces between the air molecules, and air molecules are always moving. The molecules are constantly hitting each other and hitting the sides of the soft drink bottle. When a molecule hits another molecule or the side of the bottle, it is called a collision. When air gets colder, the molecules move slower. When air gets warmer, the molecules move faster. If the volume is allowed to change then faster moving gas molecules take up more room than slower moving gas molecules.

When you put the bottle in the freezer, the air gets cold. When you take the bottle out of the freezer, the cold air gets warmer and expands. As the air warms, the molecules move faster and the collisions inside the bottle increase. Finally, the air pushes hard enough to raise the quarter and some of the air escapes. When some of the air rushes out of the bottle, you hear a click. As the air continues to warm, the quarter may jump many times.

In a fixed volume like a bottle if we increase the temperature then the pressure will increase. Pressure is the push that gas molecules exert on the walls of a container. If we decrease the temperature, the

19

pressure will decrease. When the bottle warms, the pressure increases and pushes the coin up until some of the air escapes.

Differences between hot and cold air molecules are very important in our weather. Hot air takes up more space and tends to expand and rise. Cold air takes up less space and tends to contract and fall. This rising and falling of hot and cold air is one of the main forces responsible for the winds that blow across the earth.

Other things to try

Try the experiment again and count how many jumps the quarter will make. Will it make more jumps if you cover the sides of the bottle with your hands to make it warm faster and warm more? If you use a plastic bottle, avoid pushing in the sides since this would change the volume of the bottle.

Try this same experiment with a smaller coin, like a penny or a dime. Make sure the coin covers the mouth of the bottle so the air will not escape. Does a smaller coin jump more often? Does a smaller coin jump higher?

Try a smaller bottle and see if this changes the number of jumps your coin will make. Leave your bottle in the freezer less time and see if this makes your coin jump fewer times.

DO ATOMS IN A METAL MOVE FARTHER APART WHEN HEATED?

Materials

A glass jar with a tight metal lid

Sink faucet with hot water

A towel

Procedure

Ask someone stronger than you to screw on a jar lid so tightly that you cannot unscrew it. Turn on the hot water faucet. Adjust the hot water flow to a strong, steady stream. Set the jar under the hot water so the hot water is falling on the jar lid and down the drain. Let the water run for about five minutes. Turn off the water. Dry the jar with a towel and try to unscrew the lid. Caution - the metal will be hot, but do not let it cool before you try to unscrew it.

NEVER HEAT A CLOSED CONTAINER WITH A LOT OF HEAT SUCH AS ON A STOVE. THE GLASS COULD EXPLODE DUE TO A BUILD UP OF GAS PRESSURE INSIDE THE CONTAINER.

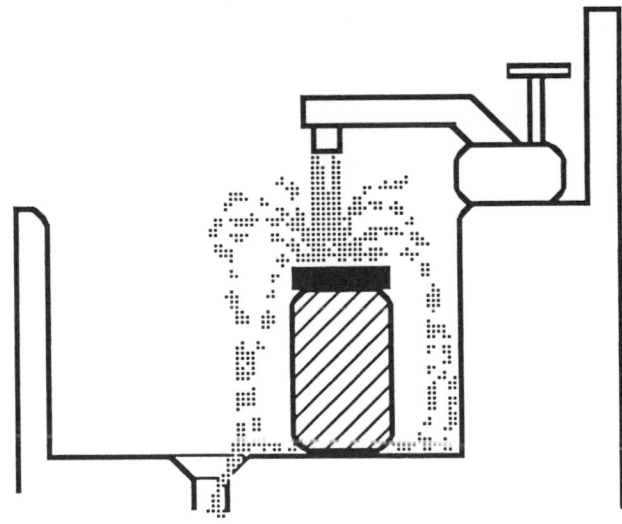

Observations

Does the jar lid feel hot? Does the glass feel hot? Can you remove the hot jar lid?

Discussion

Everything is made of atoms. The metal lid on your jar is made of atoms. Even though we cannot see atoms move, the atoms in the metal are constantly jiggling and wiggling.

Atoms move faster as they get hotter. As you run hot water on the lid, the atoms jiggle and wiggle faster and faster. As the atoms move faster, they take up more room. Therefore, the whole lid gets a little bit larger. In this experiment, the change is too small to see. However, we can feel the difference because a hot lid unscrews more easily than a cold lid. The metal gets hot faster than the glass and this makes the metal lid expand more than the glass jar.

Other things to try

Next time you have a jar with a metal lid that you cannot open, try this experiment. Are you getting stronger or smarter?

Railroad tracks have a space between the end of the rails to allow for expansion. Do you think the space between two tracks is bigger in the summer or the winter?

Metals are not the only solids that expand and contract. Other solids also get bigger when they are hot and smaller when they are cold. Look at a sidewalk. Can you explain why the sidewalk is laid with spaces between the slabs of concrete? Have you seen bridges with spaces built into them?

ARE SOME SOLIDS BETTER INSULATORS THAN OTHERS?

Materials

Two styrofoam cups

Three ice cubes of the same size

A plate

Two paper cups

Procedure

Put the first ice cube on a plate. Put the second ice cube between two paper cups stacked one inside the other. Put the third ice cube between two styrofoam cups stacked one inside the other.

Watch the ice cube on the plate. As the ice cube melts, the solid changes to liquid. Wait until the ice cube on the plate has completely changed to liquid water. Now look at the ice between the paper cups by removing the top paper cup. Next look at the ice between the styrofoam cups by removing the top styrofoam cup.

| PLATE | PAPER CUPS | STYROFOAM CUPS |

Observations

How much ice is left in the paper cup? How much ice is left in the styrofoam cup?

Discussion

Water freezes at a temperature of 0 degrees Celsius (32 degrees Fahrenheit). When the temperature is below 0 degrees, water molecules stick together and water is a solid. Solid water is ice. When the temperature is above 0 degrees, water molecules move faster and water is a liquid.

Heat flows from a warmer area to a colder area. The room is warmer than your ice cubes. Heat flows from the room air into the ice cubes. As heat flows into the ice cubes, the heat makes the molecules of water move faster. When the molecules move fast enough, they are no longer held rigidly together. The frozen water gradually changes to liquid water.

How fast heat flows depends on what surrounds the ice cube. An insulator is something that only allows a slow heat flow. More of the solid ice remains in the styrofoam cup than in the paper cup. Therefore, the styrofoam is a better insulator. The heat energy from the room air must go through the insulator to get to the ice cube.

A conductor is something that allows a fast flow of heat. Metals are very good conductors.

Other things to try

Repeat this experiment using more styrofoam cups. Try six cups with the ice cube in the middle. Do six cups make a better insulator than two cups?

Fill the bottom of a glass with hot water. Put a plastic spoon and a metal spoon in the water. Wait five minutes. Now feel the top of each spoon. Which spoon is hotter? Which spoon is cooler? Which spoon is a better conductor? Which spoon is a better insulator?

The bottom of the NASA Space Shuttle is covered with special tiles. These tiles are excellent insulators. They help keep the astronauts from getting hot when the shuttle is heated to a high temperature as it comes down through the atmosphere to land.

Think of examples of insulators and conductors around your home. Should a winter coat be an insulator or a conductor? Should a frying pan be an insulator or conductor? Can you think of other uses of insulators and conductors?

6 CAN WATER ACT LIKE GLUE?

Materials

  Two pieces of notebook paper
  Water

Procedure

  Hold the two pieces of notebook paper together. Do the sheets of paper stick together?

  Completely wet each piece of paper with water. Hold the two pieces of wet paper together. Do the sheets of paper stick together? Try to slide one sheet of paper off the other sheet.

  Place the stuck wet sheets of paper in a warm place to dry. A window that gets plenty of sunshine is a good place.

TWO SHEETS OF WET PAPER

Observations

  Do the sheets of paper stick together before you wet them with water? Do the sheets of paper stick together after you wet them with water? Is it easy to separate the wet sheets of paper by peeling them apart? Can you separate the wet sheets of paper by sliding one sheet off the other sheet? When the wet sheets of paper dry, do they stick together?

26

Discussion

Water molecules are <u>polar</u> and strongly attract each other. Polar molecules have a positive end and a negative end. The positive end of water molecules attract the negative end of other water molecules. When the two sheets of wet paper are brought together, the water molecules on each sheet are strongly attracted to each other. Water molecules are also attracted to paper. Paper contains molecules that have polar parts.

There is little attraction between the two sheets of paper when they are dry. This is because there is little attraction between the paper molecules of each sheet.

It is easy to unpeel the sheets of wet paper. It is difficult to separate the wet sheets by sliding one sheet off the other sheet. You must break the attraction between many more water molecules when you slide the sheets than when you peel the sheets apart.

Other things to try

Repeat this experiment using other kinds of paper. Try two pieces of paper toweling, two index cards, two pieces of cardboard, and two pieces of newsprint.

7 IS COLD WATER MORE DENSE THAN HOT WATER?

Materials

Red food coloring

Cold water

Hot water

Two clear glasses

A refrigerator freezer

An ice tray

A spoon

Procedure

Add several drops of red food coloring to a glass of cold water that is three-fourths full. Stir the colored water with a spoon. Pour the colored water in an ice tray. Place the ice tray in the freezer. Wait several hours until the colored water is frozen.

Fill a glass three-fourths full with hot water from a sink faucet. Set the glass on a table. Remove a colored ice cube from the tray in the freezer. Add the colored ice cube to the water. Watch the color in the glass.

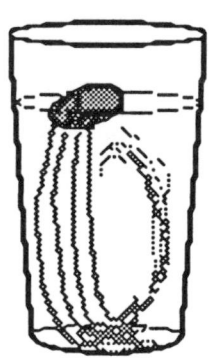

**COLORED ICE CUBE
IN WARM WATER**

Observations

Do you see streams of red color coming from the ice cube? Do the streams of color sink to the bottom of the glass? Do you see colored water on the bottom of the glass moving back to the top of the glass? Does the hot water eventually become completely colored?

Discussion

Density is a term used to compare the heaviness of the same volume of different substances. The same volume of two substances can have different weights. One cup of water weighs more than one cup of oil. Water is more dense than oil. Oil floats on water because oil is less dense than water. Ice floats on water because ice is less dense than water.

In this experiment, the colored water that forms when the ice cube melts is colder than the hot water in the glass. Cold water is more dense than the hot water. This is why streams of colored water from the ice cube sink to the bottom of the glass of hot water. The greatest density of water is at 4 degrees Celsius (39 degrees Fahrenheit). The density of water decreases as the temperature increases above 4 degrees Celsius.

The red food coloring is in the ice cube so you can see the path of the cold water. The falling cold water causes currents in the glass of water. Water currents are the movement of water in a particular path. This is why some colored water moves back to the top of the glass.

Have you ever heard of the fall overturn of lakes? In the autumn or early winter, water on the surface of a lake becomes colder and

29

more dense. The cold water sinks to the bottom of the lake. Warmer water from the bottom of the lake which is less dense rises to the surface. This movement of water in lakes is called the fall overturn.

Other things to try

Add a colored ice cube to a glass of cold water. Do you see colored water sinking from the ice cube? Does the melted colored water sink as fast as the melted colored water in hot water?

Fill a sink with cold water. Fill a small balloon with hot water. Make sure no air is in the balloon and tie it off. Place the balloon in the sink of cold water. Does it float or sink? Fill a small balloon with cold water. Make sure no air is in the balloon and tie it off. Place the balloon in the sink of cold water. Does it float or sink?

DOES SALT WATER HAVE A GREATER DENSITY THAN WATER?

8

Materials

A tall, clear drinking glass   Water

A small carrot   Salt

A teaspoon

Procedure

Fill the glass with water. Break off a piece of the carrot about an inch long. Drop the piece of carrot into the water. Now add salt a teaspoon at a time to the glass of water. Continue adding the salt until the carrot moves. You may have to add several teaspoons of salt before the carrot moves.

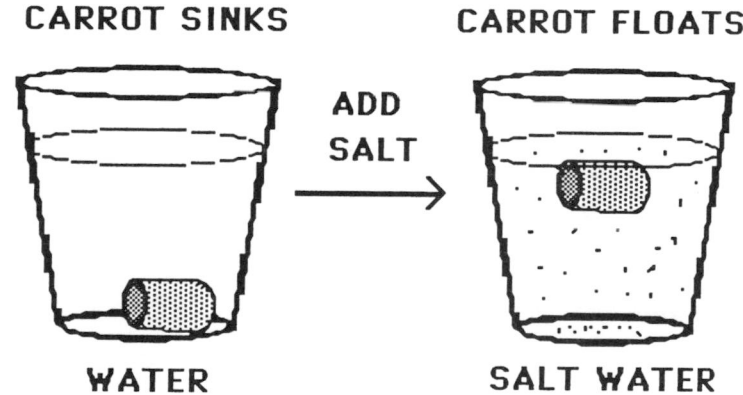

CARROT SINKS   CARROT FLOATS

ADD SALT

WATER   SALT WATER

Observations

When you drop the carrot in the water, does it sink to the bottom of the glass? As you add salt to the water, does the carrot rise? Does the carrot float to the top if you keep adding salt? How many teaspons did you add before the carrot moved to the top of the water?

Discussion

Different liquids can have different densities. The <u>density</u> of a liquid is the weight of a certain volume of liquid. If two identical glasses are filled with two different liquids, the glass filled with the denser liquid will weigh more. A heavier liquid has a greater density.

A solid that has a larger density than water will sink to the bottom of a glass of water. A solid that has a smaller density than water will rise to the top of a glass of water. Salt water is more dense than pure water. As you add salt to the water, you increase the density and the carrot rises. If you add enough salt, the carrot will float to the top of the water.

Other things to try

Repeat this experiment using bigger pieces of carrot. Do you observe the same effect? A large piece of carrot has the same density as a small piece of carrot. Density depends on what you have and not how much you have.

Repeat this experiment with different fruits and vegetables. Do different fruits and vegetables have different densities?

Try adding a piece of carrot to different liquids such as milk, cooking oil, and corn syrup. Does a carrot float in some liquids and not float in others? Can you use this observation to compare the density of different liquids?

If you have a chance to go swimming in the ocean, try floating. Because the ocean is made of salt water, you should find it easier to float in the ocean than in a pool or lake. In Utah there is a lake called the Great Salt Lake. This lake is very unusual because it is filled with water that is even saltier than the ocean. Can you explain why it is easier to float in the Great Salt Lake than in the ocean?

CAN WATER BE PURIFIED BY FREEZING?

Materials

Blue food coloring	A measuring cup
Water	A spoon
Small paper cup	A refrigerator freezer

Procedure

Pour one-half cup of water into a small paper cup. Add two drops of blue food coloring to the water. Stir with a spoon to mix the food coloring and water. Place the cup of colored water in the freezer section of a refrigerator. Leave the cup in the freezer overnight. The next day tear the paper cup from the large ice cube. Look at the ice carefully.

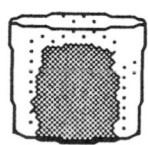

FROZEN COLORED WATER

Observations

Is the top of the large ice cube clear or colored? Are the sides of the large ice cube clear or colored? Where is most of the blue food coloring located?

Discussion

Water <u>freezes</u> at 0 degrees Celsius (32 degrees Fahrenheit). When water freezes, water molecules pack closely together in a tight pattern. Ice crystals start to grow on the surface of water first. The ice crystals grow layer by layer until all the water is a solid.

33

When you freeze colored water, only water molecules on the surface pack together in a tight pattern to form ice crystals. Food coloring molecules have a shape different than water molecules and do not pack next to solid water molecules easily. Food coloring molecules are pushed away from the growing ice crystals. This is why the top and the sides of the large ice cube should be clear. As the ice crystals continue to grow, it becomes harder to prevent the food coloring molecules from packing next to solid water molecules. The food coloring molecules become trapped in the ice crystals. This is why most of the food coloring should be seen near the center and the bottom of the large ice cube.

This experiment demonstrates <u>crystallization</u>. When a liquid changes from a liquid to a solid, it crystallizes. Crystallization is one technique used by chemists to separate a mixture of different molecules.

Other things to try

Add ten drops of food coloring to one-half cup of water. Freeze the colored water. Is the top of the large ice cube clear or colored? It is harder to prevent the food coloring molecules from packing close to the solid water molecules in the growing ice crystals because there are many more food coloring molecules present in the water.

CAN LARGE CRYSTALS BE
MADE FROM SMALL MOLECULES?

Materials

Water	A stove
Sugar	A piece of string
Two tablespoons	A pencil
A small saucepan	A paper clip
A tall, clear glass	A ruler
A measuring cup	Scissors

Procedure

ASK AN ADULT TO HELP YOU WITH THIS EXPERIMENT. DO NOT USE THE STOVE BY YOURSELF.

Pour one-half cup of water into a small saucepan. Heat the saucepan on the stove until the water boils. Turn off the heat. Add one cup of sugar to the hot water. Stir for about one minute. If all the sugar dissolves (disappears), add another tablespoon of sugar to the hot water. Stir for about thirty seconds. Let the sugar solution cool for thirty minutes.

Pour the cooled sugar water into a tall, clear glass. Try to avoid transferring any undissolved sugar to the glass. Cut a piece of string about three inches longer than the height of the glass. Tie one end of the string around the pencil. Tie the other end to a paper clip. Place the string in some water to wet it. Rub some table sugar on the string. Lower the end of the string with the paper clip into the sugar solution. Rest the pencil on the rim of the glass. Put the glass in a place where it will not be disturbed. It is important not to move the glass or string during the experiment. Watch the crystals grow every day. The longer you leave the string in the sugar solution, the larger the crystals become. It will take several days for the crystals to start growing.

To save the crystals, remove the string from the sugar solution. Gently rinse the crystals with cold water for a few seconds. Hang the string so the crystals can dry.

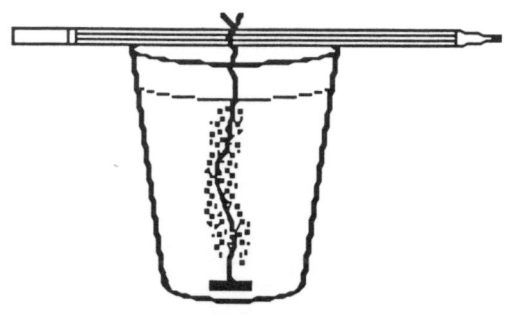

SUGAR CRYSTALS
GROWING ON STRING

Observations

How long does it take for crystals to start growing on the string? Do the crystals get bigger each day? Are there many crystals on the string? Are there crystals on the side and the bottom of the glass? Can you see through the larger sugar crystals?

Discussion

The chemical name for table sugar is <u>sucrose</u>. Look closely at some table sugar. You will see that table sugar is made of small crystals. Each crystal contains many sucrose molecules packed closely together. The sucrose molecules are strongly attracted to each other in the sugar crystal. When sugar crystals dissolve in water, the water molecules cause the sucrose molecules to break away from each other. Water molecules attract and surround the sucrose molecules. Energy is needed to break sucrose molecules away from each other. Hot water dissolves more sugar than cold water because hot water has more energy.

In this experiment you added sugar to one-half cup of hot water until no more sugar dissolved in the water. The solution is said to be saturated with sugar. When the saturated solution cools, the water molecules can no longer keep sucrose molecules from attracting each other. The sucrose molecules start to closely pack next to each other in a specific pattern. The crystal grows as more sucrose molecules pack next to each other. This packing together of molecules in a pattern is called crystallization.

The sugar crystals which were rubbed on the string provided a starting place for the large crystals to grow. These sugar crystals are called seed crystals. It is possible to grow sugar crystals without seed crystals, but it might take longer for the crystals to grow.

Other things to try

Repeat this experiment but do not rub any sugar on the string. Does it take longer for the sugar crystals to start growing on the string?

Can food coloring molecules fit in a sugar crystal? To answer this question, make a sugar solution as before. Add several drops of food coloring to the sugar solution. Stir with a spoon to mix the food coloring and sugar solution. Place a string that has sugar rubbed on it in the sugar solution. Watch the crystals grow. Remove the crystals and gently rinse them off with cold water. Is there any food coloring in the large sugar crystals? You should see colorless sugar crystals. Only sucrose molecules, not food coloring molecules, will fit in the crystal because only the sucrose molecules pack tightly next to each other.

CAN CHARCOAL REMOVE MOLECULES FROM WATER?

Materials

A measuring cup	Water
A teaspoon	Red food coloring

Two small jars (baby food jars are a good size)

Activated carbon (used in fish aquarium filters)

Procedure

Fill a measuring cup with one-half cup of water. Add eight drops of red food coloring to the water. Stir until the color is well mixed. Now, add one-quarter cup of the colored water to each of the two jars. Add two teaspoons of activated carbon granules to one of the jars. Activated carbon (charcoal) is sold in pet shops. Some brands of activated carbon are more effective than others in removing molecules from water.

Tighten the lids on both jars. Set the jars in place where they can stay for several days. Check the color of the water each day for at least four days.

CHARCOAL REMOVING DYE MOLECULES FROM WATER

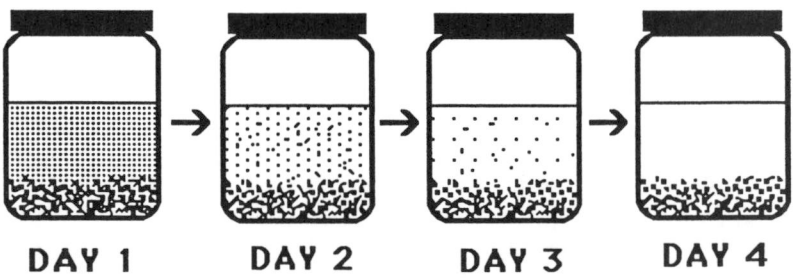

DAY 1   DAY 2   DAY 3   DAY 4

Observations

Was the color in each jar the same at the start of your experiment? Does the color of the water in the jar with the charcoal get lighter each day? Does the food color disappear from the water? Does the color of the water in the jar without the charcoal stay the same?

Discussion

The jar with no charcoal should stay the same color. However, the colored water in the jar with the charcoal should get lighter each day. The food color must be leaving the water.

Food coloring is made of <u>dye</u> molecules. Dye molecules are much bigger than water molecules. Different types of dye molecules are used to make different colors.

The dye molecules leave the water and stick on the carbon granules. Water molecules do not stick on the charcoal. The charcoal granules are made of <u>carbon</u> atoms. Because of a special treatment with steam called <u>activation,</u> the tiny pieces of charcoal have many cracks and crevices. The surface of the charcoal is very rough and has many places for dye molecules to stick. This special type of charcoal is called <u>activated</u> <u>charcoal</u> or activated carbon. This is not the same type of charcoal used in outdoor cooking. The charcoal used for cooking should not remove dye molecules from water

<u>Adsorption</u> occurs when molecules are removed from a liquid or gas and stick on a solid. Adsorption can be used to purify water and air. Many water companies use charcoal to clean water. Special charcoal filters are also used in many homes to clean water for drinking. Activated carbon is used to help keep the water in fish

tanks clean. During World War I, activated carbon was used in gas masks to remove poison gas molecules from the air.

Other things to try

Repeat this experiment using less charcoal. Does the amount of charcoal change how fast the dye molecules are removed? Does the amount of charcoal change how much food coloring can be removed?

Repeat this experiment using different colors of food coloring. Is there any difference in how well different types of dye molecules are adsorbed?

Repeat this experiment using sixteen, twenty-four, and thirty-two drops of food coloring. Is there a limit to how much food coloring can be removed from the water by the charcoal?

CAN SALT REMOVE WATER FROM THE AIR?   **12**

Materials

Salt   A small cup

Water   A tablespoon

A plastic bowl with a tight-fitting lid

Procedure

Sprinkle one tablespoon of salt into the dry bowl. Fill a small cup half full with water. Place the cup of water in the center of the bowl. Attach the tight-fitting lid on the bowl. Briefly open the lid each day for several days and observe what changes take place. Be sure to replace the lid on the bowl immediately after you make your observations.

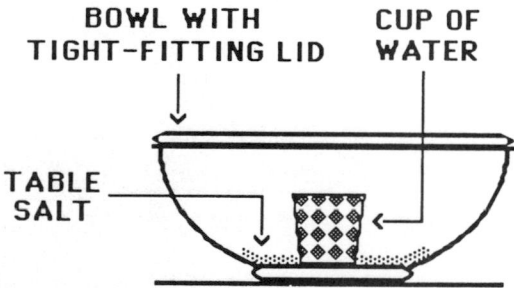

Observations

Does the salt stick together after the first day? Do you see drops of water around the salt after the first day? Does the salt look like it is getting wetter each day? Do you see more droplets of water around the salt each day?

Discussion

Air is made of mostly nitrogen and oxygen molecules. Air also contains some water molecules. The water molecules in air are a gas.

In this experiment, a bowl of air becomes filled with water molecules. Water <u>evaporates</u> from the cup of liquid water and the gaseous water molecules spread throughout the bowl of air. When water evaporates, liquid water molecules become a gas.

Some substances can remove water molecules from air. They are called <u>hygroscopic</u> <u>substances</u>. Salt is hygroscopic. Salt removes water from the air in the bowl because water molecules are attracted by the salt. Salt crystals stick together when they absorb water molecules. When salt removes water molecules from the air, more liquid water molecules in the cup evaporate and become gaseous. After a couple of days you see water droplets around the salt in the bowl. Salt can remove enough water from the air to form a salt water <u>solution</u>. Salt dissolves in water. Salt seems to disappear when it dissolves in water. A salt water solution is made when salt dissolves in water.

Have you ever noticed that it is difficult to shake salt from a saltshaker on humid days? Humid air contains many gaseous water molecules. The salt in the shaker removes water molecules from the humid air. This causes the salt crystals to stick together.

Other things to try

Can table salt that has removed water from the air be dried? To find out, remove the cup of water from the bowl. Place the bowl without the lid attached in a window that gets plenty of sunshine. Is the salt dry after a couple of days. Can you explain why?

See if other substances are hygroscopic. Try sugar, flour, baking powder, cornstarch, and baking soda. Are they hygroscopic?

CAN ADDING EPSOM SALT TO WATER MAKE THE WATER COLDER? 13

Materials

A paper cup	Epsom salt
A bowl	Water
A measuring cup	A spoon

Procedure

Add one-fourth cup of water to the paper cup. Add one cup of water to the bowl. The water in bowl and cup should be at room temperature - not hot and not cold. Put your finger in the cup and bowl to feel that the temperature of the water is the same. Add one-half cup of Epsom salt to the water in the paper cup. Stir the Epsom salt and water with the spoon. DO NOT EAT EPSOM SALT.

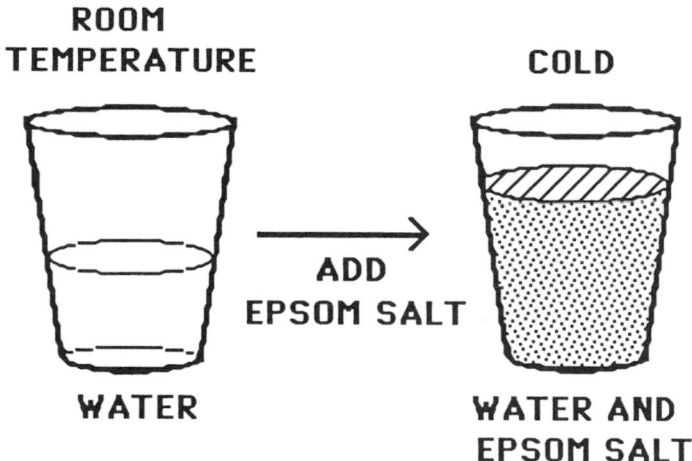

ROOM TEMPERATURE   COLD

ADD EPSOM SALT

WATER   WATER AND EPSOM SALT

Observations

Put one of your fingers in the bowl of water. Now put the same finger in the cup with Epsom salt and water. Does the water in the cup feel colder?

Discussion

Epsom salt is magnesium sulfate. Epsom salt is not used on food. Epsom salt is used for soaking sprains and bruises. When magnesium sulfate is placed in water, it breaks into positive magnesium ions and negative sulfate ions.

Heat energy can be produced. Heat energy can also be used. A chemical change that gets hot is called exothermic. A chemical change that gets cold is called endothermic. An exothermic change produces more heat than it uses. An endothermic change produces less heat than it uses. When you add magnesium sulfate to water, it gets cold. This change is endothermic.

Energy is used to break apart magnesium and sulfate ions. Energy is given off when the water molecules cluster around ions in water. Adding Epsom salt to water makes the water become cold. The water gets cold because more energy is used than is given off.

Other things to try

Repeat this experiment using table salt (sodium chloride) or baking soda (sodium bicarbonate) instead of Epsom salt. Does the sodium chloride get cold like the magnesium sulfate? Does the baking soda get cold like the magnesium sulfate? Depending on the kind of salt added to water, the water may become colder, warmer, or stay the same. You may want to try using a ziplock plastic bag instead of a cup to mix the salt and water.

See if you can find a cold pack sold in a drug store. These special packs get cold when chemical reactions take place inside the pack. These packs are used on sprains and bruises. See if the pack identifies the chemicals it uses. Try one and feel how cold the pack gets.

44

DO PLASTIC BAGS TEAR WHEN THEY ARE PUNCTURED?

Materials

A plastic sandwich bag   A sink

A sharpened pencil   Water

Procedure

Do this experiment over a sink. Fill a plastic sandwich bag three-fourths full with water. While holding the bag at the top, insert the sharpened pencil into one side of the bag and out the other side. BE CAREFUL NOT TO JAB YOURSELF WITH THE PENCIL.

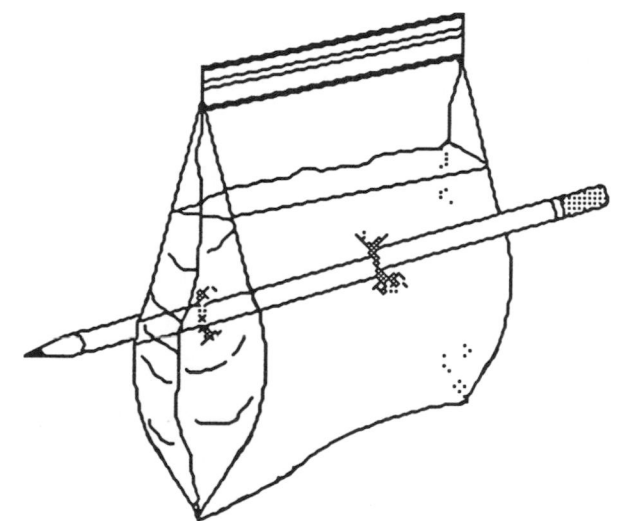

PENCIL INSERTED INTO POLYETHYLENE BAG FILLED WITH WATER

Observations

Does the plastic bag of water burst when the sharpened pencil is inserted into the bag? Does the bag tear where the pencil is inserted into the bag? Does water leak from the plastic bag where the pencil is inserted into the bag? Does water leak from the bag when the pencil is removed from the bag?

Discussion

Most clear plastic sandwich bags are made of polyethylene. Polyethylene is a special kind of molecule called a polymer. Polymers are very large molecules and are made by joining together smaller molecules into long chains. Polymer means "many parts." The smaller molecules that are joined together to make a polymer are called monomers. Monomer means "one part." The process of joining together monomers into a polymer is called polymerization.

The monomer used to make polyethylene is ethylene. Ethylene is a molecule that contains two carbon atoms and four hydrogen atoms. Ethylene is a gas. Polyethylene is a solid. Polyethylene molecules can contain tens of thousands of ethylene molecules joined together.

A sandwich bag contains many polyethylene molecules. The long polyethylene molecules in the bag are attracted to each other and are entangled with each other like a bunch of cooked spaghetti. When the sharpened pencil is inserted into the polyethylene bag, the polyethylene molecules remain entangled and pull together around the pencil. This is why the polyethylene bag does not tear or leak.

Other things to try

Try this experiment with other small plastic bags.

DO DIFFERENT OILS BECOME A SOLID AT DIFFERENT TEMPERATURES?

15

Materials

Peanut oil	Tape
Sunflower oil	A felt pen
Two small paper cups	A refrigerator freezer
A measuring cup	

Procedure

Put a piece of tape on each cup. Use the felt pen to label one cup "peanut oil" and the other cup "sunflower oil." Make sure to write on the tape.

Pour one-third cup of peanut oil in the cup labeled "peanut oil." Pour one-third cup of sunflower oil in the cup labeled "sunflower oil." Place the two cups of oil in the freezer section of the refrigerator. Leave them in the freezer overnight. Remove the two cups of oil from the freezer and make your observations.

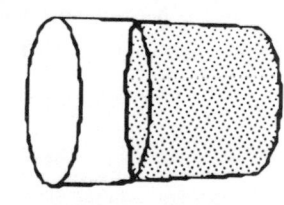

COLD PEANUT OIL

COLD SUNFLOWER OIL

Observations

Are the oils clear liquids before you place them in the refrigerator freezer? Does the peanut oil become a solid after being in the freezer? Does the sunflower oil become cloudy in the freezer? Will the sunflower oil still pour after being in the freezer?

Discussion

Fatty acids are the building blocks of oil molecules. Fatty acids are made of carbon, hydrogen and oxygen atoms. The carbon atoms in a fatty acid are joined together in a straight line. The carbon atoms are joined by bonds. Chemical bonds are what hold atoms together. There are many different types of fatty acid molecules. An oil molecule is usually made of three fatty acid molecules.

Some fatty acids contain carbon atoms joined together by double bonds. In a double bond, two carbons are joined together by two bonds. In a single bond, two carbons are joined together by one bond. Fatty acid molecules that have double bonds are called unsaturated fatty acids. Polyunsaturated fatty acids are fatty acid molecules that contain many double bonds. Poly means many. Fatty acid molecules that contain only single bonds are called saturated fatty acids.

Oil molecules do not move as fast when they are cold. Since the oil molecules do not move as fast when they are cold, the oil molecules start to stick to each other. The oil molecules become entangled in each other. The oil becomes thicker and more viscous. Substances that are viscous flow slowly. Honey is a viscous liquid.

Oil molecules that contain many saturated fatty acid molecules stick to each other more easily than oil molecules containing many unsaturated fatty acids. Oil molecules which contain many saturated fatty acids become viscous and change to a solid at a higher temperature than oil molecules containing many unsaturated fatty acids.

A substance <u>freezes</u> when it changes from a liquid to a solid. Peanut oil contains many saturated fatty acids. Sunflower oil contains many unsaturated fatty acids. Peanut oil should change to a solid when the oil is left in the freezer overnight. Your freezer should be cold enough to freeze peanut oil. Sunflower oil should not change to a solid when the oil is left in the freezer overnight. Sunflower oil has a lower freezing point than peanut oil. Sunflower oil should still pour when the oil is at the same temperature that peanut oil becomes a solid. However, if your freezer is very cold then sunflower oil can become a solid.

Other things to try

Repeat this experiment with other oils. Try olive oil, Crisco oil, corn oil, soybean oil, and safflower oil.

Is a refrigerator cold enough to freeze peanut oil? How can you find out?

Take the cup of peanut oil from the freezer and place it on a table. Does it become a liquid again after sitting on the table for several hours?

16 ARE CHEMICAL CHANGES FASTER IN HOT OR COLD WATER?

Materials

A clear glass of cold water

A clear glass of hot water

Two Alka-Seltzer tablets

Tape

A felt pen

Procedure

Place a piece of tape on each glass. Write "cold" on one piece of tape and "hot" on the other. Fill the glass labeled "cold" with cold water from a sink faucet. Fill the glass labeled "hot" with hot water from a sink faucet. Make sure the water is hot. Set each glass on a table. Add one Alka-Seltzer tablet to each glass. Watch each glass.

DO NOT DRINK THE ALKA-SELTZER WATER. Alka- Seltzer tablets are medicine and should not be taken by a child or teenager unless advised by a doctor.

Observations

Do you see bubbles in each glass? Do the bubbles form on the surface of the tablets? Do you hear a fizzing sound from the bubbles? Which glass produces bubbles more rapidly? Are both tablets disappearing? Which tablet disappears first? Which glass produces bubbles for the longest time?

Discussion

Alka-Seltzer tablets contain aspirin, citric acid, and sodium bicarbonate. Sodium bicarbonate is a salt made of positive sodium ions and negative bicarbonate ions. Each bicarbonate ion contains one hydrogen atom, one carbon atom and three oxygen atoms.

ALKA-SELTZER TABLETS
IN

HOT WATER   **COLD WATER**

When acid and sodium bicarbonate are combined in water, they produce <u>carbon dioxide</u> gas. Each carbon dioxide molecule contains one carbon atom and two oxygen atoms. This chemical reaction starts when you drop an Alka-Seltzer tablet in water.

Alka-Seltzer is <u>effervescent</u>. An effervescent substance is one that gives off gas bubbles when dropped in water. The bubbles you see are from carbon dioxide gas. The faster the reaction occurs, the more quickly bubbles appear and the faster the tablet disappears.

Hot molecules move faster and have more energy than cold molecules. Bubbles of carbon dioxide gas are produced more rapidly in the hot water than in the cold water. The tablet in the hot water disappears first because the reaction goes faster. The tablet in the cold water continues to produce gas bubbles longer because the tablet is still reacting. Chemical reactions are faster in hot water than in cold water.

Other things to try

Use some very cold water from the refrigerator and see if the reaction goes even more slowly.

Put a single drop of water on a tablet. Watch this reaction. Why does the reaction stop? Add more water and see what happens.

See how long it takes the tablet to disappear in cold water and hot water. Time the reactions. Mix equal amounts of the hot and cold water. Stir the mixture of water together. The temperature of this mixture will be between the cold and hot water. Can you predict how long the reaction will take a tablet to disappear at this temperature? Try a tablet in this mixture and see if your guess is right.

CAN MOLECULES IN THE AIR CAUSE COLORS TO FADE?

17

Materials

Red construction paper

Solid objects like coins, paper clips and pencils

Procedure

Place a piece of red construction paper in a window that gets plenty of sunshine. Place another piece of construction paper in a drawer. Set several solid objects on each piece of paper. Make sure to close the drawer containing the paper. Do not disturb the pieces of paper. Wait three days and then compare the two pieces of paper.

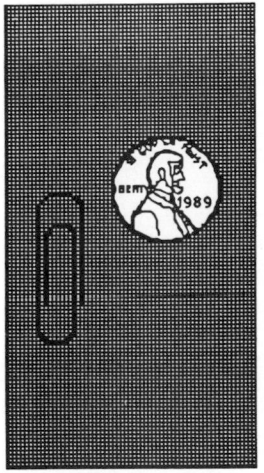

**COLORED PAPER
BEFORE EXPOSURE
TO SUNLIGHT**

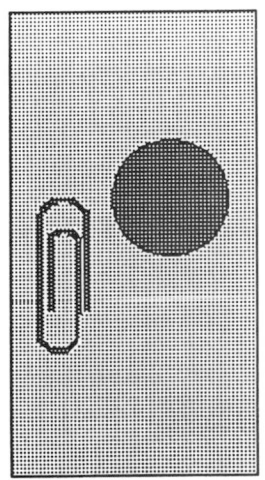

**COLORED PAPER
AFTER EXPOSURE
TO SUNLIGHT**

Observations

Does the red color in the piece of construction paper that was in the window fade except where the solid objects are? Does the red color in the piece of construction paper that was in the drawer fade?

Discussion

The red color in the construction paper placed in the window fades because of a chemical reaction. Oxygen molecules in the air react with dye molecules in the paper that give the paper a red color. The chemical reaction between oxygen molecules and the red dye molecules changes the red dye molecules. The red dye molecules are changed into molecules that are colorless or that have very little color. When oxygen molecules change other molecules in a chemical reaction the reaction is called an <u>oxidation</u> <u>reaction</u>.

Sunlight is needed for the chemical reaction to occur between the oxygen and the red dye molecules. The sunlight makes the oxygen molecules more reactive. The paper in the drawer does not fade because sunlight does not get in the drawer and make the oxygen molecules in the drawer more reactive. The red construction paper under the solid objects does not fade because the solid objects block the sunlight. The oxygen molecules are not reactive enough to change the red dye molecules under the solid objects.

Objects that sit in the sun will fade over a period of time. Have you ever seen colored curtains that have faded because of the sun and air? Look for other colored objects around your home that have faded. Some modern fabrics have special molecules in them that help slow the fading of the fabric.

Other things to try

Repeat this experiment with other colors of construction paper. Can you form the image of a leaf on a piece of construction paper? How can you do it?

CAN IRON COMBINE WITH OXYGEN AND WATER TO FORM RUST?

18

Materials

Clean steel wool

A tall, narrow jar

A large cake pan

Water

A piece of tape

Procedure

Push a loose wad of clean steel wool into the bottom of a tall, narrow jar. The steel wool should stay in place when the jar is turned upside down. Fill the pan almost full of water. Put the pan in a place where it can sit for several days without being moved.

Completely fill the jar containing the steel wool with water. Cover the mouth of the jar with your hand and quickly turn the jar upside down in the pan of water. Put your hand and the mouth of the jar under water. Remove your hand, but keep the mouth of the jar under water. The water will remain in the jar. Now lift the edge of the jar enough to let some, but not all, of the water out. As water goes out of the jar, air goes in the jar. Place the mouth of the jar on the bottom of the pan of water. Make sure you have both water and air trapped inside the jar.

Put a piece of tape on the side of the jar to mark the level of the water inside the jar. Do not move the jar. Check the level of the water each day for the next three days.

Observations

Does the water level rise inside the jar? After the third day, remove the steel wool from the jar and look at it closely. Does it look

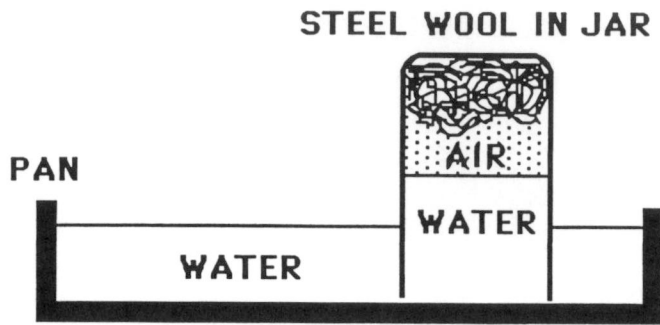

STEEL WOOL IN JAR

different from when you first put it in the jar? Do you see dark spots of rust on the steel wool?

Discussion

Steel is a metal made from iron, carbon, and small amounts of other metals such as nickel and chromium. Steel is mostly iron. Steel wool is made of long hairlike pieces of steel. Steel wool is used for cleaning and polishing.

Metals can combine with oxygen to form metal oxide compounds. These compounds contain metal atoms and oxygen atoms. One type of metal oxide is iron oxide. Iron oxide is a compound which contains three oxygen atoms for every two iron atoms. Rust is a compound that is made of water molecules and iron oxide. When iron is exposed to oxygen and water it may be changed to rust. When iron undergoes corrosion it forms rust.

Corrosion is the process where metal atoms combine with other kinds of atoms (such as oxygen) to form compounds that are not as strong as the original metal. Corrosion is a very expensive problem throughout the world. Metal in cars, bridges, ships, and buildings may undergo corrosion. It costs a lot of money to replace all the metal that is destroyed by corrosion. Have you seen an old junk car that has been destroyed by rust? One way to protect metal is to paint it so it will not be exposed to the air.

The level of water in your jar rose as oxygen molecules left the air and combined with iron atoms to form rust. About one-fifth of the air around us is made of oxygen molecules. At most, only about one-fifth of the air in your jar will be used up. Most of the rest of the air is nitrogen. The nitrogen molecules in the air do not combine with the iron atoms.

Other things to try

Repeat this experiment with a fresh wad of steel wool, but use salt water in the jar and pan instead of tap water. Is the oxygen used up faster? Does more rust form? Salt tends to make rust form faster. In northern states, salt is put on the roads in the winter to melt ice. Cars in the northern states rust faster than cars in the southern states where salt is not used as often.

Repeat this experiment with a wad of fresh steel wool, but do not let the steel wool get wet. Is less oxygen used up? Does less rust form? When a metal gets wet, the metal tends to form rust more rapidly.

19 CAN ELECTRICITY MAKE IONS THAT CHANGE NEUTRAL WATER TO A BASE?

Materials

Red cabbage leaves

A large bowl

Hot water

A measuring cup

A small jar (a baby food jar is a good size)

A piece of insulated wire (about ten inches long)

A 6-volt lantern battery

Two paper clips

Salt

Procedure

ASK AN ADULT TO HELP YOU WITH THIS EXPERIMENT. ELECTRICITY CAN BE DANGEROUS. NEVER PUT HOUSE CURRENT (electricity from a wall outlet) IN WATER. YOU SHOULD USE ONLY A SMALL BATTERY FOR THIS EXPERIMENT. DO NOT LET ANY FLAME GET NEAR YOUR EXPERIMENT.

Tear several red cabbage leaves into pieces about the size of your thumb. Put one cup of the cabbage pieces into a bowl. Add four cups of hot water from a sink faucet to the bowl. Let the leaves sit in the water about ten minutes. The water will turn purple. When the water is no longer hot, remove the leaves, and fill a small jar with the purple water. You can save your extra purple cabbage juice for additional experiments.

Connect one paper clip to the negative (-) terminal on the battery. Bend the paper clip so it sticks down into the purple water in the jar. Ask an adult to remove about one-half inch of insulation from each end of the wire. Connect the wire to the second paper clip. Put this paper clip over the edge of the jar and into the water. You need to have at least an inch of each paper clip under the water. Connect the other end of the wire to the positive (+) terminal on the battery.

Now begin to sprinkle salt into the jar of water. Continue sprinkling the salt until bubbles are constantly forming at the negative paper clip. You may have to add an amount of salt equal to about two or three teaspoons of salt. If you don't see any bubbles then you have a loose wire, bad connections, or a dead battery. Check all the wires and check your battery. Let the electricity flow through the water until the water changes color. LET THE ELECTRICITY FLOW THROUGH THE WATER FOR ONLY A FEW MINUTES SO THAT JUST A SMALL AMOUNT OF HYDROGEN GAS IS PRODUCED.

+ −

6 VOLT
LANTERN
BATTERY

PURPLE
TO
BLUE

Observations

What color is the water when you first begin to sprinkle salt? After you sprinkle salt in the water, do you see bubbles forming around the negative paper clip? Does the water change color? What is the new color?

Discussion

An <u>acid</u> is a substance that gives a positive <u>hydrogen ion</u> (H+) to water. A hydrogen ion is a hydrogen atom with its only electron taken away. A <u>base</u> is a substance that gives a <u>hydroxide ion</u> (OH-) to water. A hydroxide ion is made from a hydrogen atom, an oxygen atom, and an extra electron. A hydrogen ion and a hydroxide ion can combine to make a water molecule. A water molecule has two hydrogen atoms and one oxygen atom.

Some molecules, like those in the juice from a red cabbage, can be used to identify other molecules as acids or bases. These identifying molecules are called indicators because they will change color. Cabbage juice is red in acid and blue in a base. A solution that is not strongly acid or base is said to be neutral. Cabbage juice is purple in neutral water.

At the negative paper clip, electrons flow into the water. The negative electrons combine with water to form hydrogen gas and hydroxide ions. The bubbles you see are made of hydrogen gas. You cannot see hydroxide ions. But you know they are being made because the indicator turns blue. In a base cabbage juice is blue and not purple.

You have to add salt to make the reaction occur because the extra sodium and chlorine ions are needed to help carry electricity from the negative to the positive paper clip. Electrons flow from the positive paper clip back to the battery.

Other things to try

Can you change your blue cabbage water from a base back to neutral cabbage water? Try adding an acid such as lemon juice or vinegar to the blue cabbage water. Did the water turn purple?

Add still more acid and see if you can make the water turn red. Now what kind of ions do you have in the water?

Other colored vegetables can be used to make indicators. Try to make an indicator from grape juice, cherries, onions, beets, apple skins, or tea. Will these indicators change color with electricity?

ARE THERE CARBON DIOXIDE MOLECULES IN YOUR BREATH?

20

Materials

Two jars with lids	A measuring spoon
Water	Tape
A measuring cup	A felt pen
Pickling lime (available in the food canning section of the grocery store)	

Procedure

Place a piece of tape on each jar. Use the felt pen to label one jar "A" and the other jar "B." Pour one cup of water into jar A. Add one-quarter teaspoon of pickling lime to the water in the jar. DO NOT GET ANY OF THE PICKLING LIME IN YOUR EYES OR ON YOUR SKIN. PICKLING LIME CAN HARM YOUR EYES AND IRRITATE YOUR SKIN. Put the lid on jar A. Shake the jar for about thirty seconds. Set the jar on a table and let the undissolved (solid) pickling lime settle to the bottom of the jar. It may take several hours for it to settle. DO NOT TASTE OR DRINK THE LIMEWATER (THE WATER IN JAR A).

Use a measuring cup to carefully transfer one-quarter cup of the limewater from jar A to jar B. Avoid transferring any of the undissolved (solid) pickling lime from jar A to jar B. Put the lid on jar B. Shake jar B for about fifteen seconds. Is the limewater in jar B clear or cloudy?

Place jar B on a table and remove the lid. Keeping your mouth about six inches away from the mouth of jar B, blow about five breaths of air into the jar. Attach the lid. Shake the jar for about fifteen seconds. Now is the limewater in jar B clear or cloudy?

Set jar B on a table and leave it there for several hours.

When you have finished the experiment carefully rinse out jar A and B with water.

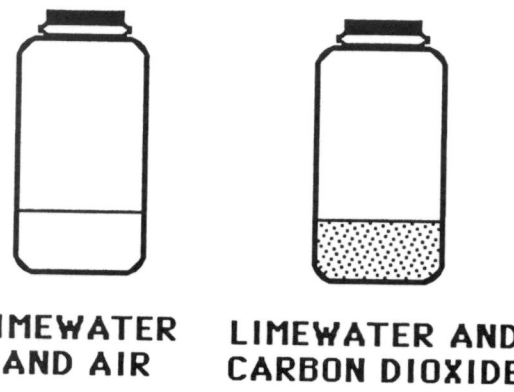

LIMEWATER AND AIR　　**LIMEWATER AND CARBON DIOXIDE**

Observations

Do you see a clear or cloudy solution when you shake one-quarter cup of clear limewater with air? Do you see a clear or cloudy solution when you breathe in the jar with the limewater and then shake it? Does this cloudy solution become clear after standing several hours?

Discussion

Pickling lime is the chemical <u>calcium hydroxide</u>. When calcium hydroxide dissolves in water, it breaks into positive calcium ions and negative hydroxide ions. <u>Ions</u> are atoms or groups of atoms that contain a positive or negative charge. A water solution of calcium ions and hydroxide ions is called <u>limewater</u>. Limewater is clear. Only some of the pickling lime dissolves in water. The undissolved pickling lime settles to the bottom of the jar as a solid.

A chemical reaction occurs when carbon dioxide molecules mix with water and calcium ions. This chemical reaction makes <u>calcium carbonate</u>. Calcium carbonate is a white solid and does not dissolve in water. Writing chalk is one form of calcium carbonate.

<u>Air</u> contains mostly nitrogen and oxygen molecules and much less carbon dioxide molecules. There are not enough carbon dioxide molecules in a jar of air to make limewater cloudy. This is why when you shake limewater with air you still see a clear solution. When you breathe into the jar of limewater, you add many carbon dioxide molecules to the jar. When you shake the jar, the water becomes cloudy. The carbon dioxide in the jar reacts with water and calcium ions in the limewater to make calcium carbonate.

Why are there carbon dioxide molecules in your breath? Your body obtains energy by combining oxygen with food molecules in chemical reactions. Food molecules contain many carbon atoms. When carbon atoms combine with oxygen atoms, carbon dioxide molecules are made.

Other things to try

Is carbon dioxide produced when you mix baking soda and vinegar? To answer this question, add one tablespoon of vinegar to one-quarter teaspoon of baking soda in a tall glass. When the mixture stops bubbling, carefully tilt the glass over a jar containing one-quarter cup of clear limewater to get some of the gas above the liquid into the jar. Do not pour any liquid in the jar. Attach the lid. Shake the jar for about fifteen seconds. Is the limewater clear or cloudy?

Does 7-Up contain carbon dioxide? It should since it is a carbonated beverage. A carbonated drink is one that has carbon dioxide gas dissolved in it. To test if 7-Up does contain carbon dioxide, add a tablespoon of 7-Up to one-quarter cup of limewater. Does the limewater become cloudy?

To show that air does contain some carbon dioxide molecules, pour one-half cup of limewater in a glass. Leave the glass on a table for several days. Do you see a white crust form on the surface of the limewater? This crust is calcium carbonate. How does it form?

CAN CREAM BE CHANGED INTO BUTTER?

21

Materials

A clean jar with tight-fitting lid

Whipping cream

A refrigerator

Procedure

Keep the whipping cream in a refrigerator until you are ready to use it. This experiment may not work well unless the cream is cold. Pour the cold whipping cream into the jar, but do not fill the jar more than a third full. Tighten the lid on the jar. Shake the jar up and down rapidly for about ten minutes. If you get tired, you can stop and rest and then shake some more. You might want to get a friend to help you. When you get a solid, shake the jar some more and then pour off the watery liquid.

You can keep your butter in a refrigerator. You can use your butter just like store-bought butter.

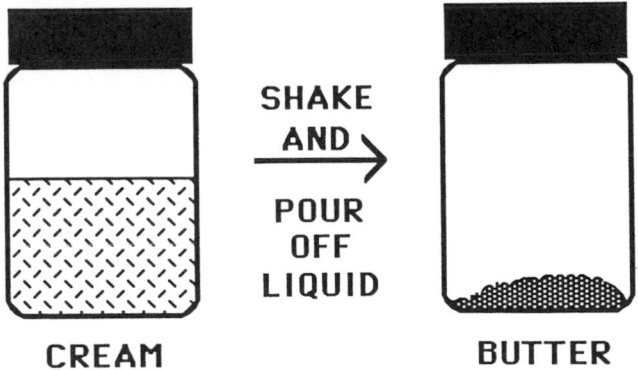

CREAM   SHAKE AND POUR OFF LIQUID →   BUTTER

65

Observations

What color is whipping cream? Is it a liquid? As you shake the cream, does it get thicker? Does the cream change to a yellow solid? Smell it. Does it smell like butter? Taste it. Does it taste like butter? Butter bought in a store may have a saltier taste because salt is frequently added to butter.

Discussion

Cream is a mixture of water molecules and <u>butterfat</u> molecules. The butterfat molecules are grouped together in tiny balls that are spread throughout the water. The tiny drops of butterfat are suspended in the water just like dust is suspended in the air. They move around, but they do not get together. However, when you shake the whipping cream, the drops bump into each other. As the drops bump, they stick together.

The drops of butterfat grow larger and larger as you continue to shake the jar. Finally, all the butterfat molecules stick together and you have a yellow solid. This yellow solid is butter. Now you can pour off some of the water that was in the cream. However, not all the water molecules are out of the butter. Some of the water molecules are trapped in the butter.

Other things to try

Repeat this experiment using skim milk instead of cream. It should not work with skim milk because skim milk contains very little butterfat.

Dip one finger in cream and rub one finger on butter. Run water on both fingers. Is it harder to wash off the cream or butter? Does the butter feel greasy?

Like molecules attract like molecules. Polar molecules have a negative and a positive side. Nonpolar molecules do not have a positive and negative side. Butterfat molecules are nonpolar. Water molecules are polar. The fat molecules in butter are not attracted by water molecules so it is hard to wash butter off your finger.

When more people lived on farms and owned cows, many people made their own butter. They made butter by churning cream collected from milk. Ask a grandparent or other older person if they ever made butter. Show them how you make butter. Find out how they used to make butter.

Do you usually use margarine or real butter? Real butter is made from cream. Margarine is made from vegetable oil and is used as a substitute for real butter. For most people real butter tastes different than margarine.

22 CAN ACID MOLECULES CURDLE MILK?

Materials

A measuring cup

A plate

A tablespoon

Milk

Lemon juice

Procedure

Pour one-fourth cup of milk onto a plate. Add two tablespoons of lemon juice. Wait five minutes then stir the mixture. Wait five more minutes and look carefully at the milk in the plate. Slowly pour off the liquid and see what is left on the plate.

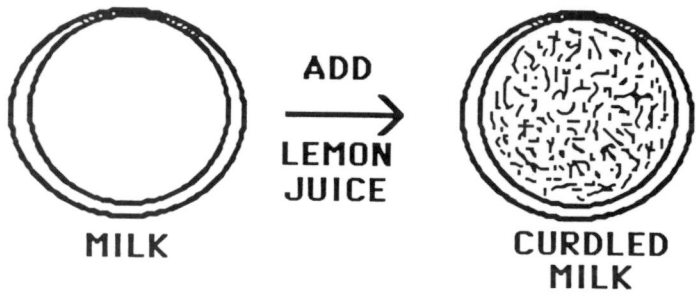

Observations

Is milk a smooth, white liquid? After you let your lemon juice and milk mixture set, is the milk still a smooth, white liquid? Do you see clumps of white mushy solid in the liquid? When you pour off the liquid, are there clumps of solid left behind?

Discussion

Milk is a complex mixture of water, sugar, fat, and protein molecules. Protein molecules are long chain molecules made by combining small amino acid molecules together like beads on a string. These long protein molecules are grouped together and coiled into small balls which are spread throughout the milk. It is these small balls that give milk its white color.

Lemon juice contains citric acid. An acid can cause the protein molecules to uncurl or spread out. The molecules spread out as if you took a wad of tangled string and stretched it straight. With the chains unraveled, the protein molecules can attach to each other and form larger clumps of molecules. The tiny balls that are too small to see can group together to form large mushy clumps of protein molecules.

This process of causing large clumps of protein to form is called curdling. When milk is curdled, curd and whey are formed. The curd is the thick lumpy part. The whey is the thin watery part. Milk can be curdled by acid or by using a special chemical called rennet. Rennet is obtained from the stomach of slaughtered calves.

The first step in making cheese is to curdle milk. Next the curd is separated from the whey. The whey is thrown out, used as an animal feed, or sometimes dried and added to other foods. The curd is used to make cheese. Microorganisms are allowed to grow in the curd to change it to cheese. Even thousands of years ago people knew how to curdle milk and use the curd to make cheese.

Other things to try

Repeat this experiment with other acids such as pineapple juice, grapefruit juice, and vinegar. Can these acids be used to curdle milk?

Have you ever tasted cottage cheese? Does it look like the clumps you formed? The lumps in cottage cheese are curd.

23 CAN BAKING SODA TRAP ODOR MOLECULES?

Materials

Two jars with lids   A tablespoon

Baking soda

Butter (use real butter and not margarine)

Procedure

Put two tablespoons of fresh butter in each jar. Smell the butter. Add two tablespoons of baking soda to one of the jars. Put the lid on each jar. Tighten the lids on the jars. Set the two jars in a warm area. Wait three days and then open each jar. Smell each jar.

Observations

Does fresh butter smell bad? Does the old butter without baking soda smell bad? Does the old butter with baking soda smell bad? Which butter smells the worst? Which butter smells the best?

Discussion

When butter is not kept cool, it can spoil. Spoiled butter is <u>rancid</u>. Something that is rancid has a very bad odor. When something is rancid, it stinks. When butter spoils, chemical reactions occur that produce <u>butyric acid</u>. Each butyric acid molecule has four carbon atoms, eight hydrogen atoms, and two oxygen atoms. Butyric acid is the molecule that causes the smell of rancid butter. Butyric acid is also found in sweat.

Baking soda is a base. An acid and a base can neutralize each other. Butyric acid molecules are neutralized and absorbed by baking soda. After the butyric acid molecules are absorbed, they can no longer become a gas and move into the air. This is why the jar with baking soda and spoiled butter should not smell rancid. The jar without baking soda is filled with butyric acid molecules. The butter in that jar should smell rancid.

Other things to try

Can you explain why it is good for us that spoiled food has a bad odor? Can you explain why some people put an opened box of baking soda in their refrigerator?

Repeat the experiment with jars kept at two different temperatures. Does the warmer butter spoil faster and smell worse?

Repeat the experiment and use less baking soda. Is there a minimum amount of baking soda needed to remove most of the butyric acid molecules?

Repeat the experiment with onion and baking soda in one jar and just onion in another jar. Does the baking soda remove onion odor molecules from the air?

24 CAN THE ACID IN LEMON REDUCE FISH ODOR?

Materials

Two small pieces of fresh fish

Water

Lemon juice

A spoon

A measuring cup

A cup

A bowl

Procedure

Pour one-half cup of water from the measuring cup into a cup. Pour one-half cup of water into the bowl. Add one-fourth cup of lemon juice to the bowl. Stir the mixture of lemon and water. Put one piece of fish in the cup and one piece of fish in the bowl. Wait ten minutes and remove the fish from the cup and from the bowl. Smell each piece of fish.

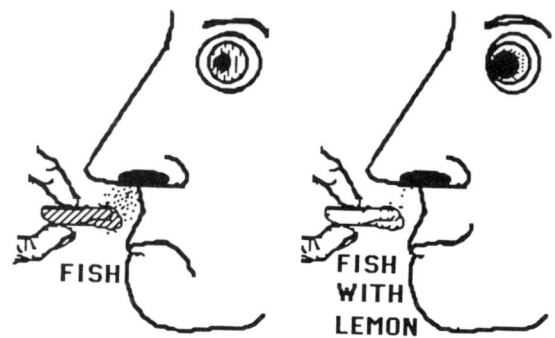

FISH

FISH WITH LEMON

Observations

Does the piece of fish from the cup have a strong fish odor? Does the piece of fish from the bowl have a strong fish odor? Which piece smells more "fishy"?

Discussion

The fish that was soaked in the cup of water should smell "fishy." The fish that was soaked in the bowl of lemon water should not smell "fishy."

Fish odors are caused by molecules that have a strong smell associated with them. These odor molecules are <u>amines</u>. Amines contain two hydrogen atoms attached to a nitrogen atom. This nitrogen atom is attached to the rest of the amine molecule. The amine molecules from fish must become a gas and go through the air to your nose before you can smell them.

An acid can contribute a proton (positive hydrogen atom) to an amine. When this positive hydrogen atom is added to the nitrogen in the amine, it changes the neutral amine molecule to a positive molecule. Three hydrogens atoms are now attached to the nitrogen. Because the amine molecules now have positive charges, fewer amine molecules go into the air to become a gas. The charged amine molecules stay in the water and on the fish. Water molecules have a negative and positive part, so they attract charged molecules.

Lemon juice is acidic because it contains <u>citric acid</u>. Citric acid causes the amine molecules to become charged. The charged amines stay in the water and on the fish and less fish odor reaches your nose.

Other things to try

Can you explain why many people squeeze lemon on fish before eating it?

Repeat this experiment with grapefruit juice, vinegar, or pineapple juice. These all contain edible acids. Do they all help to prevent amine odor molecules from reaching your nose?

Repeat this experiment using less acid. Does this make a difference in the smell of the fish?

In some restaurants when you eat fish or lobster, you are given a bowl of lemon water to dip your fingers in at the end of the meal. Can you explain why?

IS VINEGAR NECESSARY
TO DYE EGGS?

25

Materials

Four hard-boiled eggs	A two-cup measuring cup
Red food coloring	Measuring spoons
Hot water	Tape
Vinegar	A felt pen
Four cups	Four spoons
A paper towel	

Procedure

Put a piece of tape on each cup. Use the felt pen to label the cups "one teaspoon vinegar," "one-half teaspoon vinegar," "one-fourth teaspoon vinegar," and "no vinegar." Make sure to write on the tape.

Add four teaspoons of red food coloring to a two-cup measuring cup. Carefully fill the two-cup measuring cup with hot water from a sink faucet. Stir the colored water with a spoon.

Pour one-half cup of the colored water into each of the labeled cups. Add one teaspoon of vinegar to the cup labeled "one teaspoon vinegar." Stir with a clean spoon to mix the solution. Add one-half teaspoon vinegar to the cup labeled "one-half teaspoon vinegar." Stir with a clean spoon to mix the solution. Add one-fourth teaspoon vinegar to the cup labeled "one-fourth teaspoon vinegar." Stir with a clean spoon to mix the solution.

Use a spoon to place one hard-boiled egg in each of the four cups. Leave the eggs in the cups for fifteen minutes. Remove the eggs with a spoon and place them on a paper towel to dry. Observe how much food coloring is on each egg.

Observations

Is the egg that was in the cup labeled "one teaspoon vinegar" a darker red color than the other eggs? Is the egg that was in the cup labeled "no vinegar" a lighter red color than the other eggs?

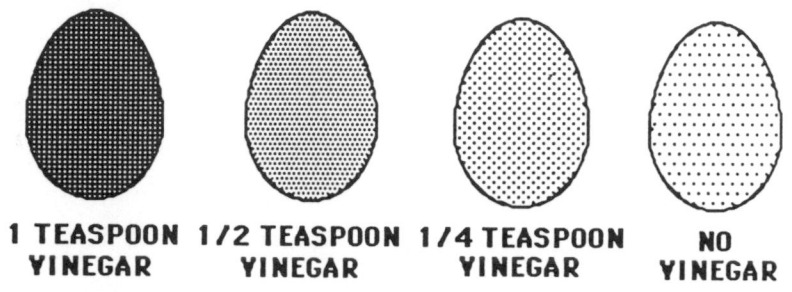

1 TEASPOON VINEGAR   **1/2 TEASPOON VINEGAR**   **1/4 TEASPOON VINEGAR**   **NO VINEGAR**

Discussion

The egg dyed in the red food coloring solution containing one teaspoon of vinegar should be darker red than the other eggs. The egg dyed in the red food coloring solution containing no vinegar is lighter red than the other eggs. These results show that vinegar is important in the dyeing of eggs and that the darkness of a dyed egg increases with increased amounts of vinegar.

When an egg is dyed, food coloring molecules stick to a layer of molecules on the surface of an eggshell. The layer of molecules on the surface of an eggshell are <u>protein molecules</u>. Protein molecules are very large molecules made by living organisms. Living organisms make many different kinds of protein molecules. The protein molecules on the surface of an eggshell help protect the eggshell. This protein layer is called the <u>cuticle</u>. The hard material under the cuticle consists mostly of the chemical <u>calcium carbonate</u>.

76

Vinegar is a mixture of water and acetic acid. Acetic acid can react with protein molecules. This chemical reaction causes many positive charges to form on protein molecules. The number of positive charges that form on protein molecules increases with increased amounts of acetic acid.

Food coloring molecules are negatively charged. Oppositely charged particles attract each other. Negatively charged molecules are attracted to positively charged molecules. In this experiment, chemical bonds form between the negatively charged food coloring molecules and the positively charged protein molecules. More food coloring molecules bond to the egg in the cup labeled "one teaspoon vinegar" because the cuticle protein molecules have more positive charges. Fewer food coloring molecules bond to the egg in the cup labeled "one-quarter teaspoon vinegar" because fewer positive charges are created on the cuticle protein molecules. Still fewer food coloring molecules bond to the egg in the cup labeled "no vinegar" because vinegar is not present to make many positive charges on the cuticle protein molecules. The amount of food coloring molecules that bond to the surface of eggshell increases with increasing amounts of vinegar.

Other things to try

Repeat the experiment using other food colorings. Do you get similar results?

26 ARE MOLECULES ON THE SURFACE OF EGGSHELLS NECESSARY TO DYE EGGS?

Materials

A hard-boiled egg	A one-cup measuring cup
Red food coloring	Measuring spoons
Hot water	A cup
Vinegar	A paper towel
A piece of sandpaper or a fingernail file	

Procedure

Rub a spot about the size of a penny on a hard-boiled egg with a piece of sandpaper or a fingernail file. You will need to rub for about thirty seconds. Place the egg in the cup.

Add one teaspoon of red food coloring to a measuring cup. Add one teaspoon of vinegar to the measuring cup. Fill the measuring cup to the one-half cup mark with hot water from a sink faucet. Carefully stir the colored water with a measuring spoon.

Pour the colored water into the cup containing the egg. Leave the egg in the colored water for fifteen minutes. Remove the egg with a measuring spoon and place the egg on a paper towel to dry. Observe the color of the egg.

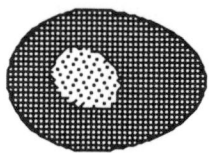

**EGG DYED IN FOOD COLORING
AFTER A SPOT WAS RUBBED
WITH SANDPAPER**

Observations

Does the egg have a spot where there is little color? Is this the spot which was made with the sandpaper? Is the rest of the egg a darker color than the spot?

Discussion

Eggshells are made mostly of the chemical <u>calcium</u> <u>carbonate</u>. Covering the surface of the calcium carbonate eggshell is a thin layer of <u>protein</u>. Proteins are very large molecules made and used by living organisms. The protein layer that covers an eggshell helps protect the egg. This protein layer is called the <u>cuticle</u>.

When an egg is dyed, food coloring molecules form a chemical bond with the cuticle protein molecules on the surface of the eggshell. Food coloring molecules are negatively charged. The cuticle protein molecules have many positive charges in vinegar. The negatively charged food coloring molecules are attracted to the positive charges on the cuticle protein molecules. A bond forms because opposite charges attract.

When the egg is dyed, very little food coloring bonds to the spot that was rubbed with the sandpaper. The sandpaper removed the cuticle protein. When the cuticle is removed, calcium carbonate is exposed. Not as many food coloring molecules stick to the calcium carbonate as stick on the cuticle. Because less food coloring molecules stick to the calcium carbonate, the color is dull and pale. The cuticle protein is necessary for eggshells to dye well.

Other things to try

Do the experiment again using other food colorings. Do you get similar results?

Soak a hard-boiled egg in vinegar for one hour. Remove the egg from the vinegar. Lightly scrub the surface of the egg while holding the egg under a stream of water. Can you see and feel a film on the surface of the egg? Does the egg have a rough or smooth surface?

Add one teaspoon of red food coloring to a measuring cup. Add one teaspoon of vinegar to the measuring cup. Fill the measuring cup to the one-half cup mark with hot water from a sink faucet. Carefully stir the colored water with a measuring spoon.

Pour one-half cup of the colored water into the cup containing the egg soaked in vinegar. Leave the egg in the colored water for fifteen minutes. Remove the egg with a measuring spoon and place the egg on a paper towel to dry. Observe the color of the egg.

Soaking an egg in vinegar partially removes the cuticle of an eggshell. Vinegar is a mixture of water and acetic acid. The acetic acid loosens the cuticle protein from the surface of the egg. You can feel and see part of the cuticle protein when you lightly scrub the egg in the cup labeled "vinegar" under a stream of water. When the egg dries, the surface is rough feeling and dull looking. The cuticle protein makes the surface of an egg smooth and shiny. When the egg soaked in vinegar is dyed, the color on the egg is dull and spotty. This is because the cuticle protein is partially removed.

The bubbles that form on the surface of the egg which is soaked in the vinegar are carbon dioxide gas bubbles. Carbon dioxide gas is one of the products formed during the chemical reaction between calcium carbonate and acetic acid.

CAN MOLECULES MOVE THROUGH A MEMBRANE?

Materials

Two cups	Vinegar	Water	Tape
Two uncooked eggs	Light corn syrup	A spoon	A felt pen

Procedure

Place an uncooked egg in each cup. Cover the eggs with vinegar. Let the eggs soak in the vinegar for twenty four hours. You need to soak the eggs until the shell is gone and the eggs are soft. Some eggs will take longer than twenty four hours.

Remove the eggs from the cups with a spoon. Pour the vinegar down the drain and rinse each cup with water. Carefully rinse each egg with water. The surface of the eggs is fragile and can easily break. Gently place each egg back in a cup. Place a piece of tape on each cup. Write "water" on one piece of tape and "corn syrup" on the other. Fill the cup labeled "water" with water until the egg is covered. Fill the cup labeled "corn syrup" with clear corn syrup until the egg is covered. You will observe changes after a few hours. More dramatic changes will be observed the eggs soak overnight.

Observations

Do you see bubbles form on the surfaces of the eggs when the eggs are covered with vinegar? Do the eggs float or sink in the vinegar? Can you see the orange yolk in the egg after the shell has been removed by the vinegar?

Does the egg in the water get larger or smaller after several hours? Does it float or sink? After several hours, does the egg in the corn syrup get bigger or smaller? Does it float or sink?

Discussion

Eggshells are made mostly of the chemical calcium carbonate.

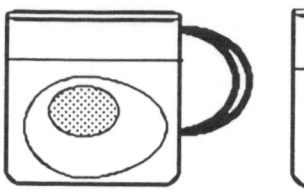 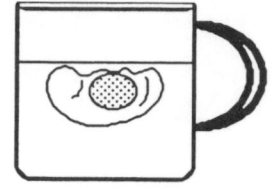

**DECALCIFIED EGG
IN WATER**   **DECALCIFIED EGG
IN CORN SYRUP**

Eggshells can be removed from eggs with vinegar. Vinegar is a mixture of acetic acid and water. Calcium carbonate under goes a chemical reaction with acids. Calcium ions and carbon dioxide gas are two of the substances that are formed in the reaction. The bubbles you see on the surface of the eggs in the cups of vinegar are carbon dioxide gas. The carbon dioxide on the surface of the eggs causes the eggs to float. When you first put the eggs in the vinegar, they sink to the bottom.

When the eggshell has been removed, the egg is called a decalcified egg. It takes about twenty four hours for the vinegar to completely remove the eggshell. Some eggs have thicker shells than others and will take longer to decalcify.

When the eggshell is removed, you will see a thin, skin-like sac that surrounds the egg white and yolk. This sac is called a membrane. Membranes are important to all cells. Membranes act like a skin. They protect the substances inside the cells.

Membranes have small openings that certain molecules can pass through. It is important for molecules to pass through membranes. This is how cells obtain substances needed to function properly.

In the second part of this experiment we see how water molecules move through the egg membrane. In the cup labeled "water," water molecules pass through the egg membrane and into the egg causing the egg to become larger. In the cup labeled "corn syrup," water molecules inside the egg move out through the egg membrane causing the egg to shrink.

In the cup labeled "water," water molecules move through the egg membrane and into the egg to try to balance the number of water molecules on each side of the membrane. Initially, there are fewer water molecules inside the egg than in the cup of water. In the cup labeled "corn syrup," there are more water molecules inside the egg than outside initially. Water molecules move out of the egg to try to balance the number of water molecules on each side of the membrane. This process of molecules moving through a membrane is called osmosis.

Certain kinds of pickles are made by placing cucumbers in salt water. Water moves out of the cucumbers because of osmosis. This is what makes the cucumbers crisp and crunchy.

Other things to try

Place the egg that soaked in water into a cup and cover it with corn syrup. Place the egg soaked in corn syrup into a cup and cover it with water. Observe what happens. This experiment will demonstrate that the osmosis process is reversible.

Decalcify an egg as before. Measure the circumference around the center of the egg. Place the decalcified egg in a cup containing water. Measure the circumference around the center of the egg each day for three days. Does the circumference change each day?

Decalcify another egg. Place the egg in water containing several drops of red food coloring. Soak the egg in the colored water overnight. Remove the egg from the cup and rinse it with water. Hold the egg over a bowl and use a fork to puncture the egg membrane. Did the red food coloring molecules pass through the membrane?

28 CAN MOLECULES IN PINEAPPLE BREAK DOWN LARGE MOLECULES INTO SMALLER MOLECULES?

Materials

One packet of unflavored gelatin	Measuring spoons
Water	A spoon
Fresh pineapple	A fork
Canned crushed pineapple	Tape
A small saucepan	A felt pen
Two small cups	A refrigerator
A two-cup Pyrex measuring cup	A stove

Procedure

ASK AN ADULT TO HELP YOU WITH THIS EXPERIMENT. DO NOT USE THE STOVE BY YOURSELF.

Place a piece of tape on each cup. Use the felt pen to label one cup "fresh pineapple" and one cup "canned pineapple." Make sure to write on the tape.

Fill the Pyrex measuring cup with one and one-half cups of water. Add this water to a small saucepan. You will heat this water on the stove in a few minutes.

Add one-half cup of cold water to the two-cup Pyrex measuring cup. Open the packet of unflavored gelatin and pour the contents into the cold water in the two-cup measuring cup. Stir the gelatin and water with a spoon for thirty seconds. All of the gelatin will not dissolve in cold water.

Heat the one and one-half cups of water in the small saucepan on the stove until the water boils. Turn off the heat. Carefully pour the hot water into the two-cup measuring cup containing the gelatin solution. Stir for about one minute to dissolve the gelatin. Let the hot gelatin solution cool for fifteen minutes.

Pour one-half cup of the gelatin solution into the cup labeled "fresh pineapple." Use a fork to crush several small pieces of fresh pineapple. Add one tablespoon of crushed fresh pineapple to the cup labeled "fresh pineapple." Stir with a clean spoon to mix the gelatin and the fresh pineapple. Into the cup labeled "canned pineapple," pour one-half cup of the gelatin solution and one tablespoon of canned, crushed pineapple. Stir with a clean spoon to mix the gelatin and the canned pineapple. Place the two cups in a refrigerator. Leave them in the refrigerator overnight.

GELATIN, WATER AND   GELATIN, WATER AND
CANNED PINEAPPLE   FRESH PINEAPPLE

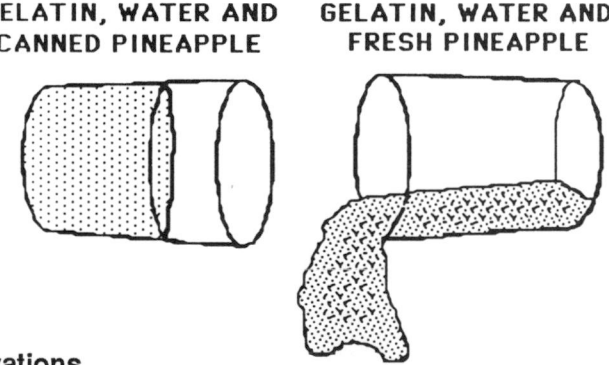

Observations

Do you get a cloudy solution when the gelatin is added to the cold water? Do you get a clear solution when the gelatin dissolves in the hot water? Does the fresh pineapple look different than the canned pineapple? Does the gelatin solution in the cup labeled "fresh pineapple" become firm and jelly-like? Does the gelatin solution in the cup labeled "canned pineapple" become firm and jelly-like?

Discussion

Proteins are very large molecules made by plants and animals from smaller molecules called amino acids. The small amino acid molecules are joined together in long chains. A protein molecule can contain thousands of amino acids joined together.

Proteins are important molecules and have many functions in living things. In the human body, proteins are the building blocks of tissues like muscle and hair. They are also the building blocks of substances that transport nutrients and oxygen in the body. Proteins are also the building blocks of enzymes. Enzymes are large, complex molecules that cause specific chemical reactions to occur in living things.

Gelatin is protein. When gelatin is added to cold water, the gelatin protein molecules pack close together. This causes light to be deflected as it passes through the solution making the solution cloudy. When hot water is added to the gelatin solution, the gelatin protein molecules are forced apart by the hot water molecules. Each protein molecule is separated by many water molecules. This is why the gelatin solution is clear. As the gelatin solution cools, chemical bonds form between individual protein molecules. This chemical bonding is called a protein network. Water molecules are trapped in the network. This makes the network flexible and jelly-like.

There are enzymes present in fresh pineapple that break down protein molecules into smaller molecules. When fresh pineapple is added to a gelatin solution, the enzymes in pineapple break down the gelatin protein molecules into smaller molecules. These smaller molecules cannot form a network. This is why the gelatin solution containing fresh pineapple did not become firm and jelly-like. Gelatin desserts cannot be prepared with fresh pineapple.

The gelatin solution containing the canned, crushed pineapple becomes firm and jelly-like. The enzymes in the pineapple were changed when the pineapple was heated in the canning process. Heat can change enzymes and make them not function properly.

Other things to try

Try other fruits to see if they contain enzymes which break down protein molecules. Try fresh figs and papaya fruit.

Ask an adult to help you boil several tablespoons of fresh, crushed pineapple in water. Add one tablespoon of the boiled pineapple to one-half cup of gelatin solution. Does the gelatin become firm and jelly-like? Does hot water change the enzyme in pineapple that breaksdown protein molecules?

Add one-half teaspoon of meat tenderizer to one-half cup of gelatin solution. Place the cup in the refrigerator overnight. Does the gelatin become firm and jelly-like?

The gelatin solution containing meat tenderizer does not congeal because enzymes in the meat tenderizer break down the gelatin proteins. Interestingly, McCormick's Meat Tenderizer is made from the enzymes found in pineapple that break down protein molecules. Adolph's 100% Natural Tenderizer contains enzymes from papaya fruit that break down protein molecules. Do you understand now how meat tenderizers make meat tender?

Congeal one-half cup of gelatin in a refrigerator. Sprinkle one-half teaspoon of meat tenderizer on the gelatin. Store the gelatin in the refrigerator overnight. Does the surface of the gelatin become watery?

29 CAN MOLECULES IN YEAST MAKE A GAS FROM HYDROGEN PEROXIDE?

Materials

Bread yeast   Measuring spoons

A bowl   A measuring cup

A solution of 3% hydrogen peroxide (available in

drugstores and some grocery stores)

Procedure

ASK AN ADULT TO HELP YOU. READ THE LABEL ON THE SOLUTION OF 3% HYDROGEN PEROXIDE CAREFULLY.

Do this experiment in a sink. Pour one-quarter cup of 3% hydrogen peroxide solution into a bowl. Sprinkle one-quarter teaspoon of yeast on the solution. Observe what happens. Stir the solution with a spoon for a few seconds. Observe what happens. Touch the bottom of the bowl. Is it warm?

Pour the 3% hydrogen peroxide and yeast solution down the sink drain. Rinse the bowl and the sink with water.

Observations

Are bubbles produced when the yeast is sprinkled on the 3% hydrogen peroxide? Are more bubbles produced when you stir the solution? Does the bottom of the bowl get warm?

Discussion

A chemical reaction occurs when yeast is mixed with hydrogen peroxide. In this chemical reaction, hydrogen peroxide molecules are changed by yeast into water molecules and oxygen molecules.

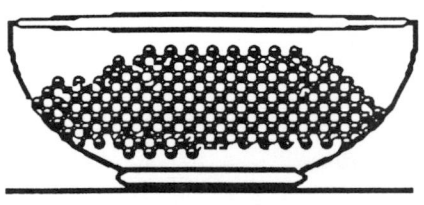

YEAST AND
3% HYDROGEN PEROXIDE

Two water molecules and one oxygen molecule are made for each two hydrogen peroxide molecules that undergo the chemical reaction with yeast. Each hydrogen peroxide molecule consists of two hydrogen atoms and two oxygen atoms. Each water molecule is a combination of two hydrogen atoms and one oxygen atom. An oxygen molecule is a tightly bound combination of two oxygen atoms.

The oxygen that is formed in the chemical reaction is a gas. The bubbles you see in the bowl of yeast and hydrogen peroxide are trapped oxygen gas.

Heat is produced when hydrogen peroxide and yeast react. The heat causes the bottom of the bowl to get warm. Reactions that produce heat are called exothermic reactions.

The molecule in yeast that reacts with hydrogen peroxide is called catalase. Catalase is an enzyme. Enzymes are large, complex molecules found in cells of living organisms. There are many different kinds of enzymes in cells. Enzymes cause specific chemical reactions in cells. The catalase enzyme in yeast cells causes water and oxygen to be made from hydrogen peroxide.

Catalase enzymes are found in the cells of most living organisms. The catalase enzymes protect cells from hydrogen peroxide molecules. Sometimes hydrogen peroxide molecules are made in cells. Hydrogen peroxide is a very reactive molecule and can harm cells by reacting with certain other molecules in the cell. This is why catalase enzymes are found in the cells of most living organisms.

Other things to try

Is the catalase enzyme changed when it reacts with hydrogen peroxide? To answer this question add a tablespoon of the 3% hydrogen peroxide solution to the yeast solution in the bowl. Oxygen gas should be produced again. This shows that the catalase enzyme in yeast is not changed in the chemical reaction.

Add a teaspoon of fresh, uncooked ground beef to one-quarter cup of the 3% hydrogen peroxide solution in a bowl. Do you see a gas bubbling from the surface of the meat? Do you think that the meat contains a catalase enzyme?

CAN SUGAR MOLECULES ROTATE LIGHT?

Materials

Two pairs of polarized sunglasses   A ruler

Light corn syrup   A small clear jar

Procedure

Add enough corn syrup (use the colorless not the dark kind) to a jar so that the syrup is two inches deep. Save this jar and syrup to use later.

Hold one pair of sunglasses in each hand. Clip-on sunglasses work well for this experiment. A bright room and a light-colored floor are best for this experiment. Close one eye and look toward the floor. Hold one pair of sunglasses about six inches from your opened eye. Hold the second pair of sunglasses about twelve inches from the same eye. Look through both pairs of sunglasses at the same time.

When the glasses are both pointing in the same direction (like II) they are said to be parallel. When the glasses are pointing cross to each other (like I_) they are said to be perpendicular.

When you hold the two glasses parallel, you should be able to look through the two pairs of sunglasses and see the ground. When you hold the glasses perpendicular and look at the ground, it should be dark. If you hold the glasses perpendicular and the light is not blocked then you do not have polarized sunglasses. You must use polarized sunglasses in this experiment.

Hold the sunglasses perpendicular so that the light does not come through and the ground looks black. While looking through the glasses have someone else hold the jar of corn syrup between the glasses. What do you see?

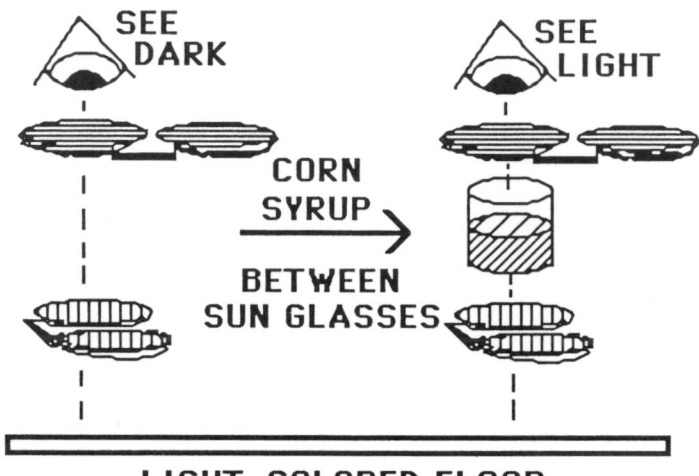

Observations

Is it dark before the jar of syrup is placed between the glasses? Does placing the jar of syrup between the glasses allow more light to get through the glasses to your eye? Can you see the floor more clearly with the syrup between the glasses?

Discussion

Polarized sunglasses are made to allow light to go through in only one direction - either up-and-down or side-to-side. Ordinary light does not have any special direction of orientation. When you hold polarized sunglasses parallel, they both let light through in the same direction. When you hold polarized sunglasses perpendicular, one lets only side-to-side light through and the other lets only up-and-down light through. Together they block out all the light.

Spread your fingers on one hand. Point your fingers up (vertical). Notice that a pencil can go through your fingers if it is pointing up but not if it is pointing sideways. Now point your fingers to the side (horizontal). A pencil can go through if it points sideways but not if it points up. Now hold both hands in front of your face with one hand pointing up, vertical, and the other hand pointing sideways, horizontal. Your hands should be perpendicular. Hold one hand behind the other. Can you see that a pencil would be stopped whether it pointed up or sideways? Can you understand why perpendicular sunglasses block all the light?

Why did the corn syrup allow some light to get through the glasses? Certain molecules can rotate light. Molecules that can rotate light are said to be <u>optically</u> <u>active</u>. Corn syrup is made from a type of sugar called <u>glucose</u> or <u>dextrose</u>. Each glucose molecule is made of six carbon atoms, twelve hydrogen atoms, and six oxygen atoms. Glucose molecules are optically active and can rotate light. The corn syrup rotates or twists the light so that some of the light can get through both pairs of sunglasses.

In 1848 a scientist named Louis Pasteur discovered that some molecules rotate light to the left and some molecules rotate light to the right. This difference in how molecules rotate light may be compared to your right and left hand.

At first your right and left hand may appear to be identical and yet you know they are different. If you place your right hand near a mirror, the image in the mirror looks just like your left hand. We could

93

say that your right and left hand are mirror images of each other. Two molecules can also be mirror images of each other and be different like your right and left hand. Molecules that are mirror images of each other can have a difference in the way they rotate light. Many important molecules in our bodies are optically active. These molecules have a "handedness" that is important in the way they function in your body.

Other things to try

While holding the corn syrup between the sunglasses, try rotating one pair of glasses and see where most of the light is blocked out. Repeat this procedure using only one inch of corn syrup. Repeat this procedure using three inches of corn syrup. As more corn syrup is used, the light should be rotated more.

As you rotate the glasses, you may see different colors of light. White light is really a rainbow of colors and you may observe this as you rotate the sunglasses. Various colors of light are rotated different amounts by the polarized sunglasses.

COMPLETE LIST OF MATERIALS USED IN THESE EXPERIMENTS

activated carbon
Alka-Seltzer tablets
apple

baking soda
balloon
beets
bowl
butter

carrot
canned, crushed pineapple
cherries
clear glasses
cooking oil
cornstarch
corn oil
Crisco Oil
cups

dime
drinking glasses

eggs
Epsom salt

felt pen
figs
fish
flour
food coloring
fresh pineapple

grape juice
grapefruit juice
ground beef

hard-boiled eggs
hydrogen peroxide,
    3% solution

ice cubes
ice tray
insulated wire

jars with lids

lemon juice
light corn syrup

meat tenderizer
measuring cups
measuring spoons
metal spoon
meter stick
milk

newspaper
notebook paper

olive oil
onions

pan
papaya fruit
paper clips
paper cups
paper towels
peanut oil
pencil
penny
pickling lime
pineapple juice
plastic spoon
plastic sandwich bags
plate
pliers
polarized sunglasses

quarter

refrigerator
refrigerator freezer
ruler
red cabbage leaves

safflower oil
salt
sandpaper
saucepan
7-Up
sink
small jars
soft drink bottle
spoons
stove
string
styrofoam cups
6-volt lantern battery
sugar
sunflower oil

table
tablespoons
tape
tape measure
tea
teaspoon
thread
towel

vinegar

water
wax paper
whipping cream

yardstick
yeast

INDEX